CW00541088

The
MELTON CONSTABLE
to
CROMER BRANCH

by
Stanley C. Jenkins, BA, PGCE, MA

THE OAKWOOD PRESS

© S.C. Jenkins & Oakwood Press 1991

ISBN 0 85361 419 9

Typeset by Gem Publishing Company, Brightwell, Wallingford, Oxfordshire.

Printed by Alpha Print (Oxon) Ltd, Witney, Oxfordshire.

An old postcard view of the sea front at Sheringham, looking east towards Beeston Hill. *Oakwood Collection*

Published by
The OAKWOOD PRESS
P.O.Box 122, Headington, Oxford.

Contents

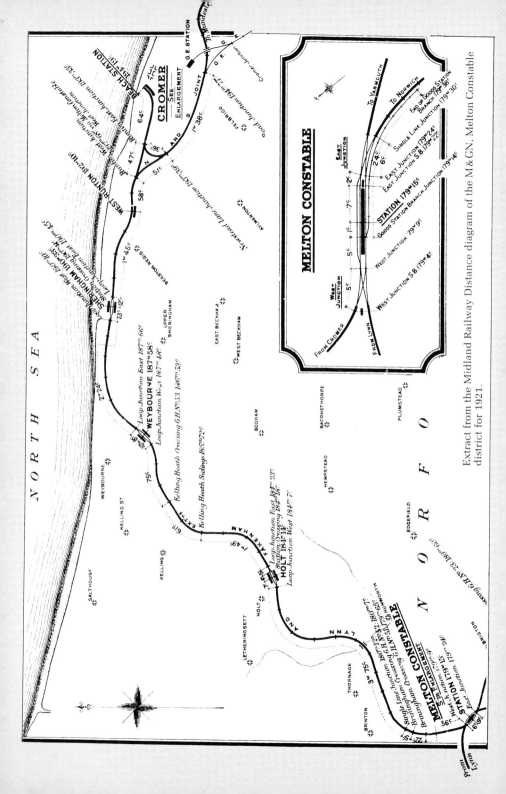

Extract from the Midland Railway Distance diagram of the M&GN, Melton Constable district for 1921.

Introduction

Branch line histories are in many respects repetitive, insofar as many English country branch lines were promoted by small groups of local entrepreneurs who, in most cases, hoped to link hitherto-isolated towns to the national railway system. Few of these lines were commercially viable, and the majority were sold to neighbouring main line companies at the earliest possible opportunity. Such lines were, by their very nature, locally-based ventures, their Directors being landowners, gentlemen farmers or professional people. The 15¼ mile branch from Melton Constable to Cromer Beach was, in contrast, an entirely different undertaking that stemmed, not from the transport needs of a local community, but from the ambitions of an unashamedly speculative venture controlled by men whose one aim was to make money for themselves. It follows from this that the history of the Melton to Cromer line does not follow the usual themes of local railway development – although the line was as fascinating as any of its counterparts elsewhere in the country.

To understand how and why the Cromer Beach line was built we must examine the general growth of rail transport in and around Norfolk between 1845 and 1880, and Chapter One of this present work will therefore explore the pre-history of the line in some detail, with special emphasis on the Lynn & Fakenham Railway – the company which, in its later guise (as the Eastern & Midlands Railway) commenced building a branch from Melton Constable to Blakeney. Chapter Two will take the story on to the completion and opening of the line which, after many vicissitudes, eventually served not Blakeney but Sheringham and Cromer. The following two chapters will then explain how this same line contributed to the growth of the north Norfolk holiday industry, first under Midland & Great Northern auspices and later as part of the LNER. Chapter Five will describe the route of the branch in detail, while the final chapter will bring the story up to date.

The *Melton Constable to Cromer Branch* is obviously a localised study but it must, at the same time, encompass the underlying history of the Midland & Great Northern Joint system and its constituents. The story of the M&GN is the essential background to the main story, and indeed the history of the Melton to Cromer line cannot be understood without at least some analysis of local railway politics. On the other hand, there is ample scope for detailed treatment of the Cromer line as a case study, and much new material will be found in the 'route' section and in other parts of this monograph.

It is hoped that the following history will be of interest to both local historians and railway enthusiasts, and that *The Melton Constable to Cromer Branch* will be a worthy companion to the author's earlier study of the rival Great Eastern branch from Norwich to Cromer.

Stanley C. Jenkins
Witney, April 1991

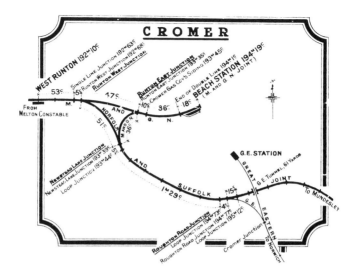

A detailed diagrammatic map of the complicated system of junctions at Cromer.

The attractive lines of a class 'C' 4-4-0, No. 17, are shown to advantage in Mr Casserley's classic view of this locomotive outside the single-road running shed at Cromer Beach on 26th June, 1929.   *H.C. Casserley*

Historical Summary

Companies of Origin

Eastern & Midlands Railway; incorporated 1st January, 1883 (by Act of 18th August, 1882) as an amalgamation of the Lynn & Fakenham, Yarmouth & North Norfolk and other companies. On 1st July, 1893 the Eastern & Midlands Railway was itself vested in the Midland & Great Northern Joint Committee – a quasi-autonomous undertaking created by the Midland and Great Northern railways to administer the former Eastern & Midlands system.

Length of Line

Melton Constable to Cromer Beach, 15 miles 16 chains.

Dates of Opening

Melton Constable to Holt (temporary terminus) – 1st October, 1884
Holt to Cromer Beach – 16th June, 1887
Runton to Mundesley (Norfolk & Suffolk Joint Line) – 23rd July, 1906 (GER); 3rd August, 1906 (M&GN trains)

Intermediate stations between Melton and Cromer

Holt, Weybourne, Sheringham and West Runton.

Mode of Operation of Single Line

Single line initially worked by train-staff-and-ticket, later by electric tablet. Intermediate crossing loops at Holt, Weybourne and Sheringham, with sections of double track at Cromer and Melton Constable. In addition, goods trains could be accommodated in Kelling Sidings while passenger trains occupied the Holt–Weybourne single line section, this method of operation being facilitated by the installation of an occupation key system.

Typical Motive Power

M&GN 'A' class 4–4–0s, 'C' class 4–4–0s, 'D' class 0–6–0s, Marriott 4–4–2Ts, Midland 0–4–4Ts, and GER 2–4–2Ts. After the LNER takeover, further ex-GER types appeared, among them 'Claud Hamilton', 4–4–0s, 'J15' 0–6–0s and 'E4' 2–4–0s.

Some Relevant Acts of Parliament

1876 Lynn & Fakenham Railway; Act of Incorporation (13th July).
1880 Lynn & Fakenham Railway; extensions to Blakeney and elsewhere (12th August).
1881 Lynn & Fakenham Railway; extension to Cromer, etc. (11th August).
1882 Lynn & Fakenham Railway; Blakeney branch deviations (11th August).
1882 Eastern & Midlands Railway; Act of Incorporation (18th August).
1888 Eastern & Midlands Railway; abandonment of Blakeney scheme (28th June).
1893 Midland & Great Northern; Act of Incorporation (9th June).
1896 Midland Railway; extension of Mundesley line to Cromer (7th August).
1898 Great Eastern/M&GN; creation of Norfolk & Suffolk Joint Committee (25th July).

A fine view of E&MR No. 15, 0–6–0ST at Melton Constable. The sister engine No. 16 (ex *Stalham*) was employed as the Melton Constable works shunter for over 30 years. This engine was painted in lined black livery, and was known locally as 'Black Bess'. *Lens of Sutton*

Chapter One
Origins of the Line (1840–1883)

Situated in the part of eastern England known as East Anglia, the county of Norfolk has always been a somewhat remote region. Yet it has never been regarded as a backward area, and on the contrary its fertile soils and close proximity to Europe ensured that, throughout the Middle Ages, the region was among the most prosperous in all England. In the 13th century, for example, Norwich was one of England's greatest provincial towns, while Kings Lynn (originally Bishop's Lynn) was one of the country's greatest ports. In 1377 the tax-paying population of Norwich was 3,952 and the corresponding figure for Kings Lynn was 3,217; these figures reveal that, after London, Bristol and Coventry, Norwich was the fourth largest town in England, while Kings Lynn was (after Lincoln and Salisbury) the seventh largest town in the country. By the 17th century, Norwich had become England's undisputed second city, its population of about 42,000 being many times greater than that of Leicester, Nottingham or other comparable towns.

East Anglia had, since the Reformation, been a staunchly Protestant region with a long tradition of thrift, sobriety and hard work. These qualities ensured that East Anglians were able to achieve prominence in many walks of life – notably banking, agriculture and the Royal Navy. By the 18th century, East Anglian banking families such as the Gurneys of Norwich had amassed great fortunes, while agriculturalists such as Thomas Coke of Holkham were already legendary; the most famous East Anglian of his day was probably Horatio Nelson – who had been born at Burnham Thorpe in 1758.

Early Railway Development in Norfolk

Inevitably, the rapid development of railways in other parts of the country during the early 19th century led to demands for a system of lines in East Anglia, and by the 1840s groups of bankers, traders and (above all) landowners were promoting a bewildering variety of locally-based railway companies. Indeed, the first East Anglian railway scheme had originated as far back as the 1820s when the pioneer railway promoter William James (1771–1837) had surveyed a possible 'engine railroad from Bishops Stortford to Clayhithe Sluice with a Branch to Waddon'. In 1824–25 an equally-grandiose 'Norfolk, Suffolk & Essex Railroad' had been projected and, if successful, this last-named scheme would have provided a viable nucleus for future East Anglian railway development.

These 1820s projects were hopelessly premature, but they served to stimulate widespread interest in the concept of rail transport and when, in the following decade, two important schemes were placed before the public the ultimate success of these ventures was assured. These two schemes were the Eastern Counties Railway (inc. 6 & 7 Wllm cap.106) and the Northern & Eastern Railway (inc. 6 & 7 Wllm cap.103). Like their abortive predecessors, the new lines hoped to link East Anglia and London but, sadly, the Eastern Counties Company was plagued by financial and other difficulties, and its promoters were forced to abandon some of their initial aims. Nevertheless, the company was able to make considerable progress at the London end of the line, and by 29th March, 1843 the ECR was open from London to Colchester, a distance of 51¾ miles.

Meanwhile, the Northern & Eastern Railway had made progress with its line between London and Bishops Stortford, and on 1st January, 1844 the Eastern Counties Railway took over the Northern & Eastern Company on a 999 year lease. The Eastern Counties main line had still not progressed beyond Colchester, but the Northern & Eastern route was pushed on to Cambridge and Brandon on 29th July, 1845; on that same day, the separate Norwich & Brandon Railway was also opened, and the two lines thereby formed a continuous chain of communication between London, Cambridge, Brandon, and Norwich. Further progress was made on 15th December, 1845 when the opening of Trowse swing bridge at Norwich enabled the Yarmouth & Norwich Railway to be linked to the new main line. A few months previous to this, on 30th June, 1845, the Yarmouth & Norwich Railway had combined with the Norwich & Brandon Company to form the aptly-named Norfolk Railway.

The Railway Mania in NW Norfolk

Noting the ease with which the Eastern Counties and other railways had been promoted, the people of north and west Norfolk were eager to promote railways of their own in order that hitherto-railwayless towns such as Kings Lynn could be joined to the growing Victorian railway system. Indeed, the bankers and traders of Kings Lynn were involved in several schemes during the 'Railway Mania' of the middle-1840s – one of the most important of these projects being the Lynn & Ely Railway which was incorporated on 30th July, 1845 with Powers to construct a 25 mile main line from Kings Lynn to Ely, together with branches to Watlington (later Magdalen Road), to Wisbech and from Kings Lynn to Lynn Harbour.

In the meantime, various other speculators were promoting lines running east and west from Kings Lynn, in the hope that these additional lines could one day link up with other railways in the Midlands and North in order to complete a useful trunk route between Yarmouth, Norwich, Kings Lynn and industrial centres such as Birmingham, Leicester and Nottingham. Much of this promotional activity stemmed from the efforts of one man – J.C. Williams, a local solicitor whose range of professional contacts ensured that he was ideally-placed to organise and co-ordinate the often disparate schemes that mushroomed during the 1840s. On 21st July, 1845, for example, the Lynn & Dereham Railway was formed to link Kings Lynn to the Norfolk Railway (8 & 9 Vic.cap. 26) while, further south, Williams was also involved with the Lynn & Huntingdon Railway. Both of these lines were – with the Lynn & Ely Railway – part of one 'grand design' which, when completed, would secure a whole network of lines in the Kings Lynn area.

Another line promoted during the hectic days of the Railway Mania was the North of Norfolk Railway which, if successfully completed, would have provided a line running from Norwich to Cromer, with a westwards continuation to Holt. The scheme was supported by the Norfolk Railway, while at the same time the latter company had projected a line to Blakeney – suggesting that these two routes might one day be linked to produce a whole series of lines in North Norfolk.

Sadly, the Railway Mania ended in unprecedented financial disaster. With so much money tied-up in railway schemes it was perhaps inevitable that the boom would be followed by a slump, but the crisis, when it came, was of unparalled severity. The first hints of trouble came with an unexpected failure of the potato crop at the end of 1845 and when, in the following year, both the corn *and* potato harvests failed, the Victorian financial system was thrown into utter confusion. By 1847, prices were spiralling and thousands of people were thrown out of work; in Ireland and Scotland – even in parts of England – people were starving to death or dying of diseases brought on by malnutrition, and against this background of social and economic disaster the railway stock market collapsed.

The North of Norfolk, the Norfolk Railway's Blakeney branch, and many of the other schemes hatched during the Mania were abandoned, but certain more important projects were hurried to completion, and in these critical years several sections of line were opened to traffic – among them the Lynn & Ely Railway which reached Downham on 27th October, 1846 and was completed throughout to Ely on 25th October, 1847. Further east, the Lynn & Dereham line was completed throughout on 11th September, 1848, while the main line from London to Colchester, and thence to Norwich, was finally completed on 12th August, 1849.

Formation of the GER – A Monopoly is Created

There had, meanwhile, been a series of important amalgamations, and, as a result, the Eastern Counties Railway had emerged as a major force in East Anglia. At the same time, the Lynn & Ely, Lynn & Dereham and Ely & Huntingdon Railways had themselves amalgamated to form the East Anglian Railway, but an attempt to merge the latter company with the ECR foundered in 1847. Nevertheless, the Eastern Counties Railway eventually gained control of all of these minor companies, and in 1862 the process by which the ECR acquired its smaller neighbours culminated in the passing of an Act to 'Amalgamate the Eastern Counties, the East Anglian, the Newmarket, the Eastern Union and the Norfolk Railway companies'. Although in effect the ECR had simply absorbed lines which it already controlled or worked, the company wisely decided to rename itself 'The Great Eastern Railway' – thereby establishing its credentials as a new organisation which would (hopefully) serve the people of East Anglia by providing cheap and efficient rail transport facilities.

The newly-created Great Eastern system was a large and monopolistic organisation which covered much of East Anglia with a comprehensive network of main line and branch railways. The company inherited two main lines from London to Norfolk, one running via Colchester (the former ECR route) while the other extended northwards via Cambridge to Kings Lynn. These two lines were linked by a variety of east to west cross-country routes which, between them, served most of the towns in Norfolk and Suffolk.

There were, by the early 1860s, still one or two gaps in the system, but it was envisaged that the missing links could be supplied by locally-based companies working in close co-operation with the GER. In the early 1860s, for example, a group of north Norfolk squires and landowners promoted the Lynn & Hunstanton Railway to build a short branch from Kings Lynn to a new holiday resort at Hunstanton, while on 23rd June, 1864 a similar company was empowered to build the 'East Norfolk Railway' between Norwich and North Walsham; these two lines were opened on 3rd October, 1862 and 20th October, 1874 respectively, the North Walsham line being later extended to Cromer.

The Lynn & Hunstanton and East Norfolk companies were both supported by the Great Eastern, and although it was assumed that both of these branches would enjoy a modicum of independence, the intention was that the two lines would work in very close conjunction with the GER – becoming in effect branches of the Great Eastern system. The thought that some entirely *independent* company would one day challenge the Great Eastern's undisputed monopoly may have crossed the minds of the GER Directors, but in the 1860s few people could have imagined that such a company would ever have been promoted. Indeed, there seemed little need for further large scale railway development in East Anglia because the existing Great Eastern network already tapped most places of any importance. There were, on the other hand, other companies active in the area to the west of Kings Lynn, and in order to understand fully the subsequent history of the Midland & Great Northern Railway it will be necessary to say a few words about these interlopers.

On 15th November, 1858 the opening of the Norwich & Spalding Railway had brought the rival Great Northern Railway into the area, and on 1st July, 1862 the original Norwich & Spalding line was extended westwards to reach Sutton Bridge. Meanwhile, the Lynn & Sutton Bridge and the Spalding & Bourne railways had been formed to extend the Norwich & Spalding route eastwards and westwards respectively. The Lynn & Sutton Bridge line was opened to traffic on 1st March, 1866, its trains reaching Kings Lynn via a junction with the Great Eastern Railway at South Lynn. Opening of the Spalding & Bourne followed on 1st August, 1866 – by which time these three local companies had amalgamated to form the Midland & Eastern Railway, the necessary Act being obtained on 23rd July.

The Midland Railway, too, was interested in the Kings Lynn area, and on 28th July, 1863 the Peterbrough, Wisbech & Sutton Bridge Railway was empowered to make a railway from Peterborough to Thorney, Wisbech & Sutton; this Midland-backed venture was opened on 1st August, 1866, from which date the Midland Railway also gained access to the GER station at Kings Lynn.

The Lynn & Fakenham Railway

These diverse lines can be seen as attempts by the Midland and Great Northern companies to penetrate East Anglia and challenge the Great Eastern's monopoly – although it would, in the event, be several years before that challenge could become really effective. In the short term a locally-promoted line – The Lynn & Fakenham Railway – appeared to pose a much greater threat to Great Eastern interests in north-west Norfolk.

The Lynn & Fakenham was a lineal descendent of earlier Railway Mania schemes that had hoped to build east-to-west cross-country lines across north Norfolk in opposition to the Lynn & Dereham Railway. Such schemes were, by their very nature, separate from the Eastern Counties/East Anglian alliance and, as such, they remained outside the Great Eastern orbit when that company was created in 1862. It follows that the Lynn & Fakenham and its progenitors were essentially rivals to the GER, and when, in the early months of 1876, the Lynn & Fakenham Bill was sent up to Parliament, it was bitterly opposed by the Great Eastern Railway and its allies.

It was hoped that the Lynn & Fakenham line would run from a junction with the Lynn & Hunstanton Railway in the parish of Gaywood to a terminal station in Fakenham – though the promoters envisaged that a connecting line would also provide access to and from the existing GER station in Fakenham. The Great Eastern, however, was understandably opposed to any links to its own system, and in presenting evidence against the Bill hostile GER witnesses claimed that there would be no room for further traffic at Kings Lynn. Many local landowners were, in contrast, in favour of the new line, and on 13th July, 1876 the Act authorising 'the construction of railways between Kings Lynn and Fakenham in the County of Norfolk' received the Royal Assent.

The Lynn & Fakenham promoters were thereby empowered to build a railway running eastwards from 'the Parish of Gaywood by a junction with the Lynn & Hunstanton line of the Hunstanton & West Norfolk Railway' and terminating 'in the parish of Hempton on the west side of the road from Raynham to Fakenham'. The authorised line would be about 19 miles long, and to pay for its construction the promoters were empowered to raise capital of £150,000 in £10 shares, together with a further £50,000 by loan. Supporters of the scheme included Lord Townsend – a major local landowner – Mr William Walker of Little Massingham, Sir W.A. Browne-Folkes, and the Reverend I.L. Brereton. As far as can be ascertained, none of these gentlemen were in any way connected with the GER, and the Lynn & Fakenham project must therefore be seen as an entirely competitive promotion.

Ironically, the Lynn & Fakenham scheme was dependent, at least to some extent, on Great Eastern co-operation, but the new company was very much a 'cuckoo in the nest' and the Great Eastern did little to smooth the path of its unwelcome guest at Kings Lynn. Although the newcomer had been granted running powers into Kings Lynn station, the GER obstructed the flow of construction materials via Gaywood Junction on the pretext that such powers applied after the opening of the L&F, but not before. Meanwhile, construction of the Fakenham line was being pressed forward at several places along the route, and in October 1878 the Lynn & Fakenham Directors announced that 2¾ miles of line had already been laid; the rails would, they hoped, be in Massingham by the end of the year.

Having successfully passed its Board of Trade inspection the Lynn & Fakenham line was opened between Kings Lynn and Massingham Road on 16th August, 1879. Diverging eastwards from the Hunstanton branch some 1½ miles from Kings Lynn station, the new railway followed the Gaywood River for 2½ miles and then crossed Roydon Common to reach Hillington – a small village to the south-east of Sandringham Park; an intermediate station was provided at Grimston Road. The line was completed throughout to Fakenham on 16th August, 1880, by which time the ambitious Lynn & Fakenham promoters had deposited a Bill seeking Powers for further extensions to Norwich and Blakeney. There was, however, considerable indecision vis-à-vis the Blakeney line, and although the L&F Directors were unwavering in their desire to reach Norwich, the company could not decide how to implement its plans for a northern extension.

The Blakeney Scheme

The initial scheme for a northern extension from Melton Constable to the coast had envisaged a branch line running northwards to Kelling Heath, at which point the route would fork, with one arm heading north-east to the coastal village of Sheringham and the other proceeding north-westwards to Blakeney – a busy fishing centre on the remote North Norfolk coast. Powers for the Blakeney branch were secured on 12th August, 1880 when the Lynn & Fakenham's ambitious extension Bill received the Royal Assent.

The 1880 L&FR Act provided consent for a variety of new lines which, for convenience, were treated as separate railways. As far as the Blakeney scheme was concerned the Act 'to enable the Lynn & Fakenham Railway Company to extend their Railway to Norwich and Blakeney, and for other purposes' referred to no less than three new lines, and these were defined as 'Railway No. 4', 'Railway No. 5' and 'Railway No. 6'.

Railway No. 4 was carefully described (with reference to the Bill) as a railway:

> Six miles, six furlongs and six chains or thereabouts in length wholly in the County of Norfolk being so much only of Railway No. 4 shown on the deposited plans as extends from the commencement thereof in the . . . parish of Melton Constable with Little Burgh by a junction with Railway No. 1 to the point shown on the said plans as six miles six furlongs and six chains from the commencement.

Railway No. 5 would commence in the parish of Kelling by a junction with Railway No. 4 and run north-westwards for a little over 4¼ miles to terminate 'in the parish of Wiveton in a meadow known as Fifteen Acre Marsh'. Finally, Railway No. 6 would continue for a further 1 mile 4 chains to reach a terminus near 'the south-west end of the quay' at Blakeney.

If successfully completed this scheme would have resulted in the creation of an 11 mile branch running north-westwards from the Lynn & Fakenham main line at Melton Constable to Blakeney. The proposed line would have served one of north Norfolk's few natural harbours, and in this context it is interesting to relate that 19th century Blakeney was an important fishing centre, over 300 boats being registered there in the 1870s. Mussel fishing was of particular importance, but the harbour was also used by oyster smacks and herring luggers.

Blakeney was in relative decline by the early 1880s, but it was hoped that a rail link would enable locally-caught fish to reach wider markets and so lead to a revival of the fishing industry; there were, therefore, good reasons why the Lynn & Fakenham promoters were keen to reach Blakeney, and it is easy to understand why Sheringham was initially regarded as a goal of somewhat lesser importance – there was, after all, no harbour at the latter place, and many local fishing craft were based in the haven at Blakeney (rather than on the exposed beaches at Cromer or Sheringham).

Meanwhile, the Lynn & Fakenham Directors were acting in close liaison with the proprietors of a small railway in the Great Yarmouth area, and when, in 1877, the first section of 'The Great Yarmouth & Stalham Light Railway' was opened to traffic, this local company was already viewed as a close ally of the Lynn & Fakenham Railway. In 1879 the Great Yarmouth & Stalham Light Railway supporters had unsuccessfully sought Parliamentary consent to amalgamate with the Lynn & Fakenham; the name of the GY & SLR Company had, meanwhile, been changed, the new title being 'The Yarmouth & North Norfolk Railway'.

The Yarmouth & North Norfolk route was opened throughout between Great Yarmouth and its western terminus at North Walsham on 13th June, 1881, and in the following year the Lynn & Fakenham Directors sought Parliamentary consent for a connecting link between their own line at Melton Constable and the Y & NNR route at North Walsham. At the same time, a similar scheme came before Parliament; known as 'The Central Norfolk Railway', this alternative project was remarkably similar to the Lynn & Fakenham scheme in that its promoters envisaged an east-to-west main line across central Norfolk from Norwich to Melton Constable, together with a northern branch line from Melton to Kelling. Here, the route would bifurcate, with one arm extending to Blakeney while the other served Sheringham and Cromer.

A Further Act of Parliament

In the event, Parliament preferred the Lynn & Fakenham proposals, and on 11th August, 1881 the Lynn & Fakenham obtained Parliamentary consent for the hoped-for link between its own route at Melton Constable and the Yarmouth & North Norfolk line; the proposed line would be 17 miles 32 chains long, and when completed it would effectively extend the Lynn & Fakenham route to North Walsham and thence, via Y & NNR metals, to Great Yarmouth.

These developments were of great importance to the Lynn & Fakenham Company, in that they represented the final links in a somewhat tenuous chain of railways extending from the Great Northern main line in the west to Great Yarmouth in the east. The resulting line incorporated three distinct undertakings, the Midland & Eastern and the Yarmouth & North Norfolk lines being the western and eastern links respectively, while the Lynn & Fakenham Railway occupied a vital position as the intervening link between these two entirely separate concerns.

Although the extensions to North Walsham and (to a lesser extent) Norwich were of immense importance to the Lynn & Fakenham, the company did not forget its proposed northern extensions, and the 1881 Act had also contained provisions relating to the Blakeney branch. While still hoping to reach Blakeney, the L & F Directors decided that a link from Kelling Heath to Sheringham and Cromer could also be built, and to facilitate this change of plan the new Act provided consent for the construction of two further railways which would, between them, extend the authorised line from Melton Constable in a north-easterly direction towards Cromer. These new lines were defined as 'Railway No. 3' and 'Railway No. 4'. Railway No. 3 was described as:

> A Railway 4 miles, 4 furlongs 1.4 chains or thereabouts in length commencing in the parish of Kelling by a junction with Railway No. 4 authorised by 'the Lynn & Fakenham Railway (Extensions) Act 1880' and terminating at or about 370 yards from the Water Fountain at Lower Sheringham measured in a south-westerly direction.

The easternmost part of the extension would carry the line towards Cromer, and this section (Railway No. 4) was described as a railway:

> 3 miles 7 furlongs 2.2 chains or thereabouts in length commencing by a junction with Railway No. 3 at the point hereinbefore described as the termination thereof, and terminating near the cemetary at Cromer.

The 1881 Act also contained numerous provisions for the protection of landowners and local residents. For instance, the railway company would have to provide 'a convenient means of access across Railway No. 3' where it crossed Kelling Heath (this meant that, in effect, the company would have to build an otherwise unnecessary level crossing or bridge across the line near Holt).

The Lynn & Fakenham company had, in the meantime, made good progress with its main line from Fakenham to Melton Constable. The new line was substantially complete by the summer of 1881, and preliminary work had commenced on a new locomotive works which the Lynn & Fakenham Directors decided to build on a site at Melton Constable. The first brick was laid in May 1881, and on 19th January, 1882 Melton Constable station was opened to public traffic, along with the L & F line from Fakenham to Guestwick (on the Norwich branch). On 1st July, 1882 the line was completed between Guestwick and Lenwade, a distance of 6 miles 10 chains.

With money and resources heavily committed to the Norwich and North Walsham lines, the Lynn & Fakenham Directors were unable to devote much time or energy to the Blakeney route. However, on 11th August, 1882 the company obtained a new Act permitting further amendments to the proposed branch. The original 1880 scheme had provided consent for a line ending near the south-west end of Blakeney quay, but it was felt that this proposal did not allow sufficient scope for an expansion of port facilities, and the 1882 Act therefore contained provision for additional lines along the southern side of Blakeney Harbour. One line would commence 'in the parish of Blakeney' by a junction with the original line and terminate 'in the parish of Stiffkey, 100 yards to the north of the public road from Morston . . . and about 1,270 yards west of the sluices on the Stiffkey Stream', while the other would extend northwards from Morston to end on the 'South Side' of Blakeney Harbour channel. Together, these two lines would add a further 4 miles 46 chains of railway to the Blakeney scheme, and provide a basis for further harbour lines or tramways to new wharves or jetties in the Blakeney area.

Further provisions in the 1882 Act allowed for the purchase of Blakeney Harbour, the sum of £5,400 being specified for that purpose. The Act also provided for the construction of new harbour works along the south side of the harbour channel – the idea being that modern port facilities would be created downstream of the original wharf so that fishing vessels or other craft could come alongside at all states of the tide.

Formation of the Eastern & Midlands Railway

Unfortunately, external events intervened before the Blakeney scheme could be brought to a successful conclusion. As we have seen, the Lynn & Fakenham Railway occupied an important place in what was soon to become a lengthy east-to-west cross-country route; the Lynn & Fakenham already worked in close liaison with the Yarmouth & North Norfolk Railway while, further to the west, the Midland & Eastern Railway had earlier been created to bring together the hitherto-diverse lines between Kings Lynn, Spalding and Peterborough. A further amalgamation would obviously confer many advantages on the enlarged system, and a complex amalgamation scheme was therefore devised. Behind this scheme was (possibly) the hand of the Midland Railway – though the wishes of individual shareholders (and indeed local pride) dictated that an outright amalgamation with the MR or Great Northern was not a viable option. Instead, the various parties involved approached Parliament for consent to form a new company, to be known as the Eastern & Midlands Railway.

The Eastern & Midlands Act received the Royal Assent on 18th August, 1882, and the Lynn & Fakenham Railway was thereby able to amalgamate with the Yarmouth & North Norfolk, the Midland & Eastern and the Peterborough Wisbech & Sutton Bridge companies. The amalgamation was, for legal reasons, carried out in two stages, the Eastern & Midlands Company being formed before the Midland & Eastern and Peterborough Wisbech & Sutton Bridge companies were formally dissolved. As far as the Lynn & Fakenham was concerned, the amalgamation became effective on 1st January, 1883; the Norwich line had been ceremonially opened on 2nd December, 1882 – thereby becoming the last section of railway to be opened under Lynn & Fakenham auspices.

The Eastern & Midlands Railway was, in many respects, merely an enlarged Lynn & Fakenham, but the 1882 amalgamation may have had an adverse effect on the Blakeney scheme insofar as the newly-formed Eastern & Midlands Railway should have turned its full attention to the Blakeney branch as soon as the main lines were in operation. However, although the Melton Constable to Norwich line was opened throughout in December, 1882 there was no attempt to implement the Blakeney project. On 5th April, 1883 the completion of the Melton Constable to North Walsham route released men and equipment for use on the northern extension from Melton to Holt, but progress was painfully slow and Blakeney residents must, by 1882, have suspected that their branch line would never be built!

In fact, the Eastern & Midlands Directors were now questioning the need for a branch to Blakeney. This was, in part, because the Eastern & Midlands already served the ports of Kings Lynn and Great Yarmouth, and in these circumstances the proposed new port development at Blakeney may have been viewed as an unnecessary extravagance. More importantly, neighbouring Cromer had developed as an immensely successful seaside resort since the opening of the Great Eastern-worked East Norfolk Railway from Whitlingham Junction (near Norwich), and the Eastern & Midlands Board clearly hoped that their own line could benefit from Cromer's rising popularity.

The Origins of 'Poppyland'

It should, perhaps, be stressed that the Cromer area had a most able publicist in the person of *Daily Telegraph* reporter Clement Scott (1841 – 1904) who had 'discovered' Cromer in the 1880s. It was, at that time, little more than a village, and having fallen in love with the area, Mr Scott proceeded to celebrate the charms of what he called 'Poppyland' in verse and prose. One of the most popular of these poems was *The Garden of Sleep* – inspired by a ruined church yard on the clifftops at Sidestrand. When the words of the poem were set to music by Isodore de Lara the resulting ballad rapidly became one of the most popular songs in circulation, and large numbers of tourists were encouraged to visit 'Poppyland' to see the 'tower in ruins' standing guard 'o'er the deep'.

Once Clement Scott had placed Cromer on the Victorian tourist's map, the potential benefits that would accrue from an Eastern & Midlands branch were obvious. A line to Cromer from Melton Constable would enable the Eastern & Midlands Railway to openly compete with the established Great Eastern route to London, but more importantly, the Eastern & Midlands route would tap entirely new markets in east Midlands towns such as Leicester and Nottingham. At the same time, the provision of a new rail link along the picturesque north Norfolk coast was likely to stimulate further resort development in hitherto-remote villages such as Weybourne and Sheringham – with the result that still more travellers would wish to visit the area.

The projected Melton Constable to Cromer branch was, by 1883, clearly seen as a worthwhile addition to the growing Eastern & Midlands system, but the E&MR Directors were still unable to reach a firm decision on the viability of the Blakeney harbour scheme. Blakeney had initially been viewed as an primary objective, the branch to Sheringham and thence to Cromer being very much an afterthought. However, the rise of Cromer as a prestigious seaside town meant that what had originally been regarded as a 'branch' soon became the most important part of the whole extension scheme, and although Blakeney remained an ultimate objective there was little attempt to begin construction. Instead, the Directors decided that preliminary work could take place at the southern end of the route between Melton Constable and Holt, and 5 miles of line were soon in place between those two points. Curiously, the works were then abandoned, and in 1883 the E&MR Company switched its attention to the planning of a direct 'cut-off' line at Kings Lynn; there was, at this time, *still* no firm decision on the Blakeney scheme.

There had, in the interim, been an important decision vis-à-vis the financing of the Cromer branch. The Eastern & Midlands Railway and its progenitors were, from their inception, mainly speculative ventures which were intended to make money for their promoters – indeed, the entire system was operated on a shoe string, loans and other expedients being resorted to in order to finance the company's various extension schemes. One of these expedients was the promotion of 'separate undertakings' as a means of attracting new preference capital, and the Cromer branch and Lynn Loop lines were both financed on this principle. In reality this system was fraught with perils, and reputable journals such as *The Railway Times* were quick to condemn the E&MR and its Directors for what was seen as a highly dubious practice.

Significantly, the composition of the Eastern & Midlands Board of Directors had undergone many vicissitudes since the 1870s, and although, in Lynn & Fakenham days the scheme had been supported by landowners such as Lord Hastings and Sir W.A. Browne-Folkes, these gentlemen subsequently resigned, leaving the management of the E&MR firmly in the hands of contractors and speculators. The new men were not interested in the provision of cheap and efficient local transport services; instead, they hoped to build a railway as quickly and cheaply as possible so that, when finished, it could be sold to some convenient main line company (hopefully for a profit). The Blakeney line, as such, did not fit into this scheme, but Cromer held out the prospect of future wealth, and local residents were, by the end of 1884, confident that the hoped-for branch line would soon be in operation!

The sea front at Cromer, looking west towards the pier (completed in 1899 at a cost of £11,000).   *Oakwood Collection*

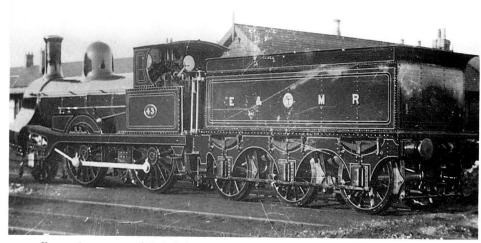

Former Lancaster and Carlisle locomotive No. 8 seen here as E & MR No. 43 at Melton Constable, probably after rebuilding in 1891. The sister engine, No. 42, ended its days working the Cromer branch pick-up freight service.   *Loco. Publishing Co.*

An early view of Beyer, Peacock Class 'A' 4–4–0 No. 24, photographed at Cromer prior to the public opening of the line.   *Loco. Publishing Co.*

Chapter Two

Construction, Opening and Early Years (1883–1901)

The Melton Constable to Cromer branch was built in stages over a period of about four years. Overall supervision of the works was the responsibility of William Marriott (1857–1943), the Eastern & Midlands' own Engineer. Mr Marriott had already carried out much work on the Lynn & Fakenham main line and other constituents of the E&MR – and he was also in charge of the company's locomotive department, being locomotive superintendent as well as civil engineer. The Resident Engineer was a Mr Stockman, and his assistant was Mr G. Gribble; the leading foreman was Samuel Shirt, who had once worked for Thomas Brassey, the well-known Victorian contractor.

The authorised route commenced at Melton Constable and dropped relatively steeply into the valley of the River Glaven, through which the new line would proceed to the market town of Holt. Having followed the valley for about 1½ miles the proposed route then climbed towards Kelling Heath, where the line would fork, with one branch heading north-west to Blakeney while the other arm continued north-eastwards to the sea near the village of Weybourne. From here, the low-lying coast afforded an easy path towards Sheringham – though the hillier terrain around Cromer would necessitate considerable engineering work for the railway builders. There were, on the other hand, no major obstacles along the 15¼ mile route, and from an engineering viewpoint, construction of the branch was expected to present few problems.

Opening to Holt

As we have seen, the 5 mile line between Melton Constable and Holt was left unfinished in 1883, but construction work resumed in the following year, and this first section of the Cromer branch was soon ballasted throughout its length. Financial considerations precluded the employment of external contractors, and in an attempt to conserve the company's meagre capital resources the Eastern & Midlands Directors decided to complete the line with their own staff and equipment. It was hoped that the Melton Constable to Holt line could be brought into use as quickly as possible, the idea being that revenue from the new line could be used to finance the construction of other unfinished parts of the Eastern & Midlands system.

William Marriott recalled that although the rails had reached Holt in 1883, there had been no attempt to begin work on the station or yard, and in order to expedite the work he brought 'the old wooden station from Yarmouth' and adapted it for use as a temporary booking office and waiting room at Holt.[1] The line itself, however, was well-constructed, and it was passed 'without difficulty' by Major-General Hutchinson of the Board of Trade. Having obtained BoT sanction, the company was able to open the Holt line to public traffic, and the first trains ran between Melton Constable and Holt on 1st October, 1884.

The Holt line was soon contributing much-needed revenue to the struggling Eastern & Midlands Railway, but when, in January 1885, the company obtained possession of the land needed for construction of a much-needed 'cut-off' line at Kings Lynn, the men who had been working on the Cromer route were set to work on the 'Lynn Loop' line. The Lynn Loop was opened for goods traffic on 2nd November, 1885 (and for passengers on 1st January, 1886) and its rapid completion ensured that, after so many delays, work could once again resume on the Cromer branch.

Construction Resumes

As usual, the Eastern & Midlands Company carried out most of the work between Holt and Cromer by direct labour, the cuttings and other earth-works being let to sub-contractors at agreed sums per cubic yard, while the station contracts were let out to local building firms. William Marriott remembered that the horses and mules used during the construction of the line were hired 'from Jacob Gray of Sheringham and Callow of Northrepps'; rails, switches and crossings were fabricated in the newly-opened works at Melton Constable, and the signalling was installed by the Eastern & Midlands' own signal and telegraph staff.

The authorised route from Holt to Cromer was heavily graded, but there was a good mix of cuttings and embankments, and spoil from the cuttings could be tipped to form raised embankments. Temporary contractor's lines were used to move excavated material along the unfinished route, the construction trains being worked by diminutive contractor's engines that had earlier worked on the Lynn & Fakenham main line.

The appearance of construction trains on the unfinished line caused quite a stir in small towns and villages such as Weybourne and Sheringham. Although the nearest railhead at Cromer was only a few miles away, many country people – particularly those of an older generation – had never seen a train before, and William Marriott mentioned that a lady known as 'Old Granny Craske' was 'got into a bath chair and taken to the level crossing to see her first engine.[2] (This anecdote serves as a reminder of how immobile many people were in pre-railway days, and one can imagine the transformation brought about in small, rural communities by the coming of railways such as the Melton to Cromer line!)

Having finally decided to complete the Cromer line, the Eastern & Midlands Directors seem to have taken a special interest in this seaside route. It was believed that the prospect of carrying lucrative 'Poppyland' traffic would encourage the Midland Railway (or some other ambitious main line company) to purchase the entire Eastern & Midlands system, and with these thoughts in mind the E&M Board wanted the branch completed without further delay. On 10th April, 1886 *The Railway Times* reported that 'the works of the Cromer line' had been commenced and arrangements were being made 'for pressing them forward so as to ensure the opening to Cromer in the spring of next year'.

Work continued unabated throughout the winter of 1886–87, and in a subsequent report, published on 9th April, 1887, *The Railway Times* announced that the works on the Cromer line were 'rapidly approaching completion'.

A few months earlier, in February 1887, an article in *Engineering* had provided a highly detailed account of the new line, and some of this interesting data is worth quoting. After describing the recent history of the Eastern & Midlands Railway, the report continued as follows:

> The new line commences at Holt, and runs for 2½ miles through a very easy country, then enters a cutting, from which some 70,000 yards of earth have been taken. From the entrance of this cutting there is an incline of 1 in 80 for two miles, which is the heaviest gradient on the whole system through a succession of cuttings and embankments; but, after this, there is but little work till near Cromer, where there is a cutting containing upwards of 80,000 yards and 40 ft deep. As Cromer lies low and is surrounded by high ground this was unavoidable. The materials excavated were ballast, &c., and at the Holt end, chalk and marl in the centre, and a mixture of many different kinds of earth at Cromer. There are stations at Holt, Sherringham, and Cromer. In all cases the stations are close to the towns, and this will give this company a great advantage over the Great Eastern Railway at Cromer, for the station is fully a mile away, and at the top of a steep hill very similar to the Ilfracombe station of the London and South-Western Railway. The line is single throughout, but the stations are made for double line; the platforms at Holt and Sherringham are 350 ft long and 12 ft wide, ample siding accommodation is provided, and arrangements made for the immediate despatch of fish by both passenger and goods trains. The platforms at Cromer will accommodate three long trains at a time, and both of them can be used for arrival or departure. The goods' yards are so laid out as to be capable of future extension, and no curve is of less than 10 chains radius for a siding, and 20 chains for a facing point junction. The radius of the curves on the main line varies from 30 to 80 chains.
>
> The Holt and Sherringham station-houses have each a general waiting-room 20 ft by 14 ft with an open pitch pine roof, a booking office 14 ft by 11 ft station-master's office 14 ft by 9 ft, and ladies' waiting-room 12 ft by 9 ft, all 10 ft high. The Cromer Station has a hall 26 ft square, a first class room 18 ft by 13 ft 6 in., a ladies' room 14 ft by 10 ft, booking-office 24 ft by 7 ft, parcels office 24 ft by 12 ft, station-master's office 14 ft by 10 ft, and porters' room 14 ft by 7 ft 6 in., all 12 ft high, and in addition a station-master's house attached and refreshment and dining-rooms with kitchen, cellar, and lavatories, and a length of 175 ft of covered platform. The roof of this platform is of a type not often seen in England, although the same class of roof is frequently used in Scotland. It is of unequal pitch, by which means the glass is placed nearly vertical and is consequently not so prone to the usual failing of flatly pitched glass roofs, namely, leakage.
>
> In designing the bridges and other works the engineer has been guided by the materials on the spot; having provided himself with a general idea of the work required, he had the set of type drawings prepared shown in Figs. 1 and 2, and these standards were kept to as much as possible. Owing to ballast being plentiful, concrete, with a brick facing, has been in many cases adopted for the abutments and wing walls. By reference to the drawings it will be seen that Fig. 3 is an over-bridge built for a double line with the wings shortened, as only a single line is at present required. It will be noticed that this type is very economical in headway, the rise of the arch being regulated by the loading gauge. This bridge contains some 80 yards of concrete and 250 yards of brickwork, and cost about £350. The coping is of bull-nosed blue brick, and all arches are turned in cement.
>
> Figs. 4 and 5 show an over-bridge close to a station where a double line is required. As headway here is very important, Lindsay's steel flooring has been adopted, the parapet being built on two rolled joists. From the surface of road to the soffit of the girders is but 18 in. This flooring has been adopted for the same

reason to economise headway on the 36 in. span girder bridge shown in Fig. 6. The flooring is here rivetted to the girders and stiffeners, and a very neat and strong job is made. The bridges shown in Figs. 7 and 8 are very cheap, where headway is of no great importance. That with a 15 ft roadway cost only £230.

A rather more elaborate form of bridge is shown in the four-arched example in Fig. 9. This is suitable for a narrow roadway where headway is of importance, although it is rather more expensive than the elliptical arch. In the under bridges of small span to economise headway and so save excavation, the rails are carried on balks in trough girders as in Fig. 11. From rail level to the soffit of the troughs is but 12 in. Fig. 12 represents a neat and inexpensive three-arch under-bridge. This has been built in red brick with arches in white relieved by blue bick in piers and imposts which produces a very pleasing effect.

The fencing consists of eight wires, two of which are the galvanised barb which forms a most effectual protection against stock.

The rails used are of the Vignoles pattern and are fastened to the sleepers by means of clips and fangs, no holes being bored in the flanges.

The line will be worked on the tablet system, which is the greatest boon to single-line working. It provides absolute security with a certain amount of elasticity in the train working, so that if one train is late, other trains that it has to cross at various stations can be brought forward. This with the old train staff was impossible, as it takes too long to shift a staff by trolley or by road.

The works have now so far progressed that it is expected that the line will be open for passenger traffic in the spring; they will thus have been in hand for little over twelve months. Nearly 1000 yards a day have at times been excavated in the cutting at Cromer, and this is now nearly finished, the bridges and station buildings are also practically finished, and eight miles of permanent way laid.

The stations at Holt and Sherringham were built by Messrs Bardell Brothers, King's Lynn, that at Cromer by Messrs Leach and Sons, King's Lynn, the bridges by Mr William Wilson, of North Walsham, and the ironwork was supplied by Messrs Barnard, Bishop, and Barnards, of Norwich. The labour also in the cuttings was sublet.

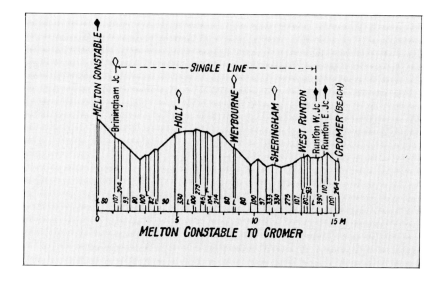

MELTON CONSTABLE TO CROMER

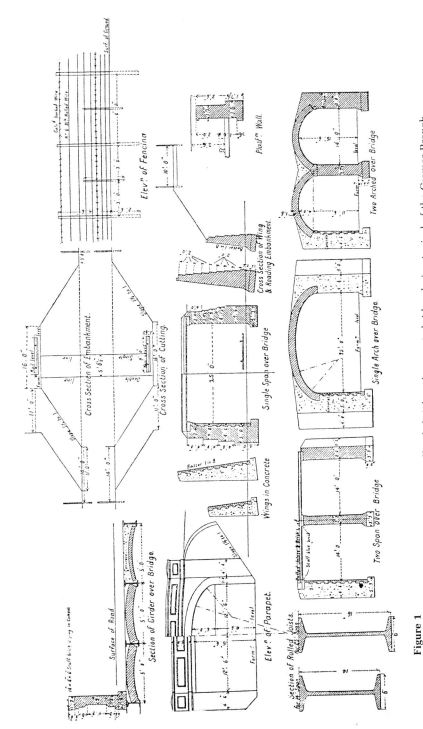

Figure 1

Some typical Eastern & Midlands brick and concrete bridge design typical of the Cromer Branch.

25

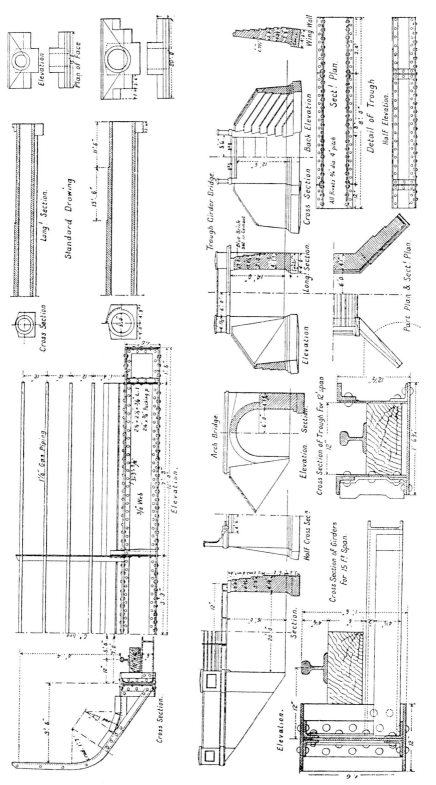

Figure 2

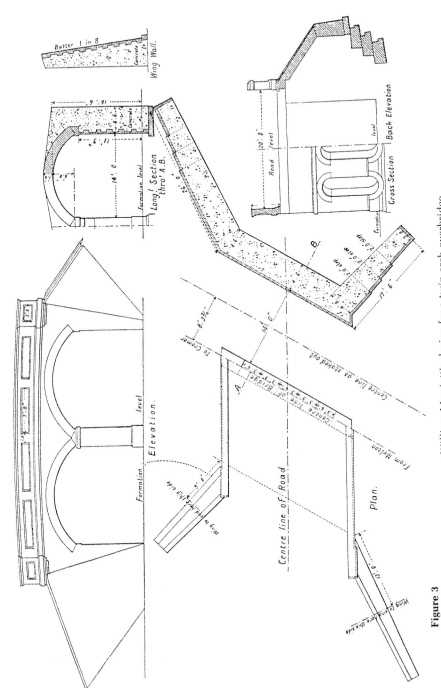

Figure 3

William Marriott's design for a twin-arch overbridge.

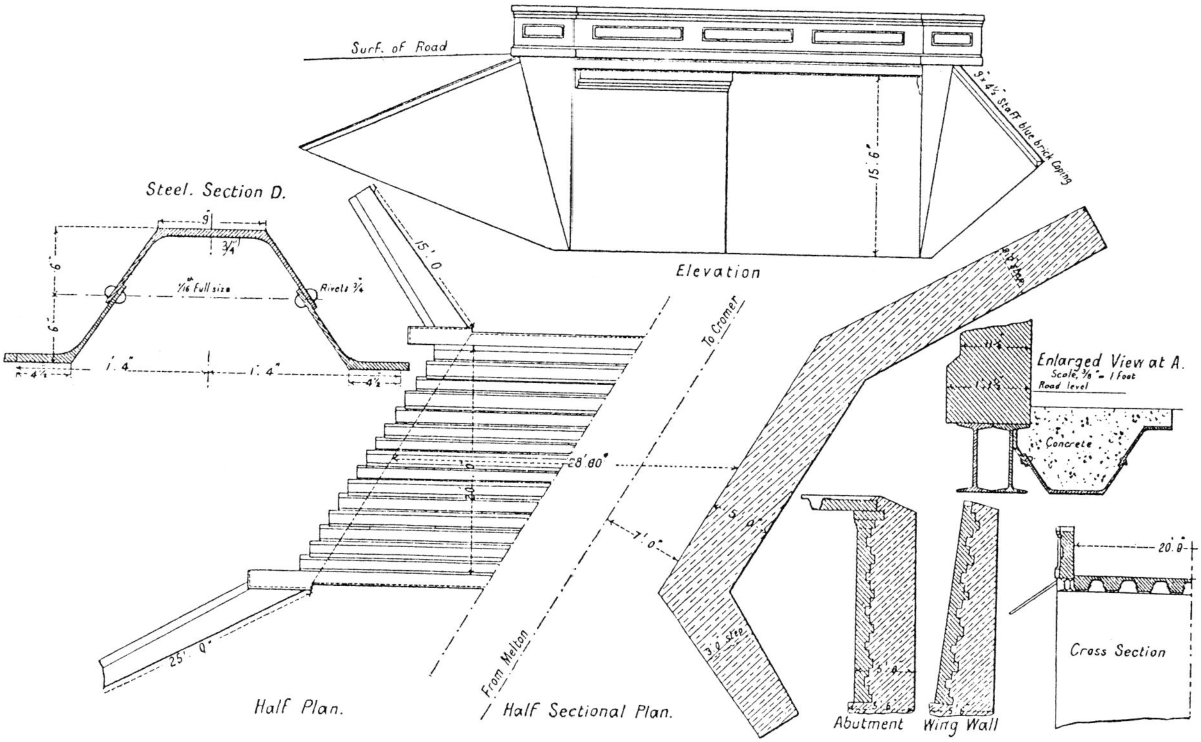
Surf. of Road
9 x 4½ Staff blue brick Coping
15' 6"
Elevation
Steel. Section D.
9
¾"
1/16 Full size
Rivets ¾
6"
1' 4"
4½
15' 0
To Cromer
28' 80"
20' 0
7' 0"
5' 0"
3' 0 step
From Melton
25' 0"
Half Plan.
Half Sectional Plan.
Enlarged View at A.
Scale, ⅜" = 1 foot
Road level
Concrete
Abutment
Wing Wall
Cross Section
20' 0"

Figure 4

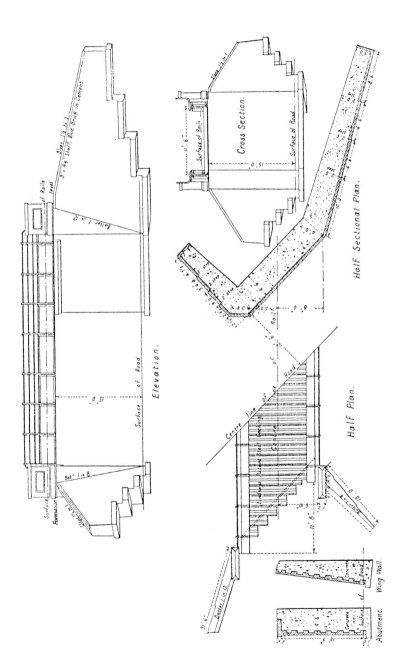

Figure 5

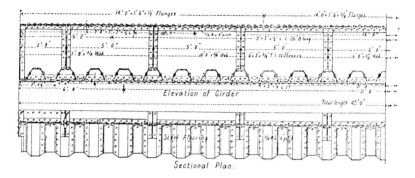

Figure 6

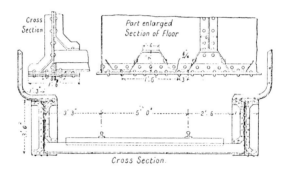

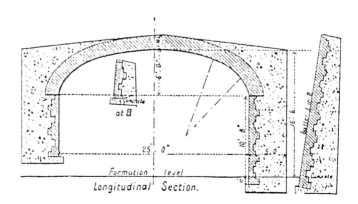

Figure 8

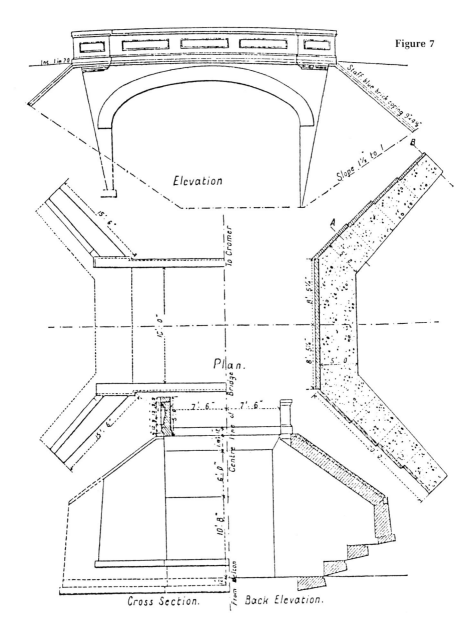

Figure 7

Elevation

Plan.

Cross Section. *Back Elevation.*

Figures 7 and 8 are examples of 'cheap' overbridges where headway is unimportant.

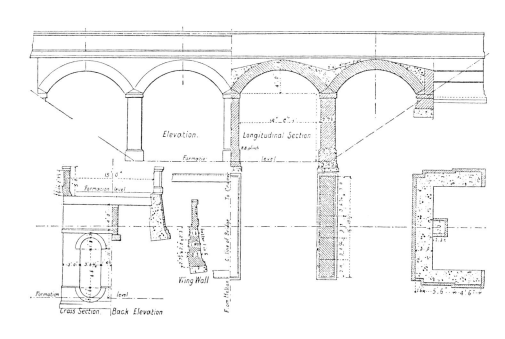

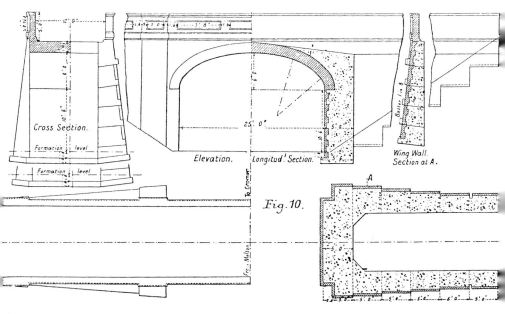

Figures 9 and 10

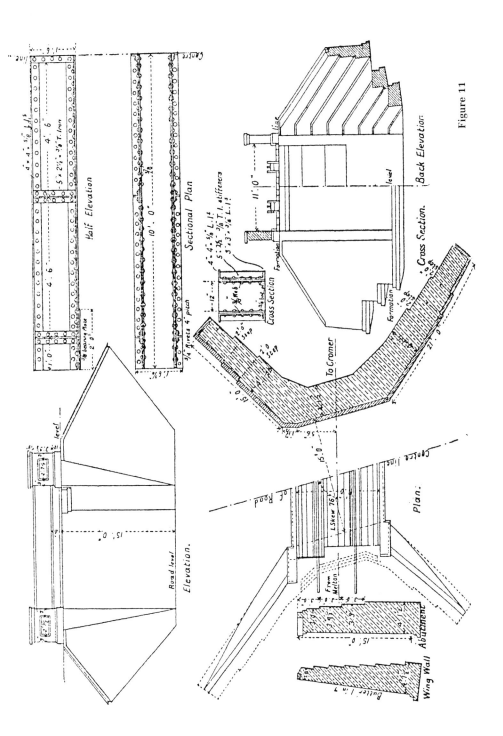

Figure 11

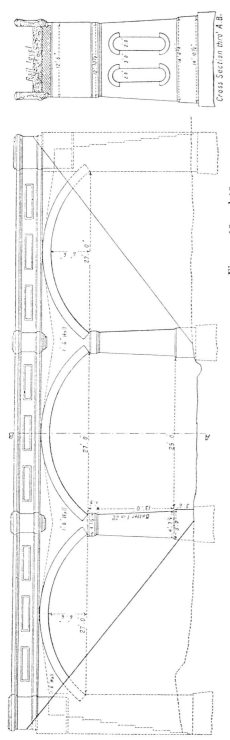

Cross Section thro' A.B.

Figures 12 and 13

William Marriott's design for a three-arched underbridge.

A view of the Viaducts near Cromer, the nearer one carrying the N&S line between Newstead Lane and Roughton Road Junction and the further one carrying the Sheringham to Cromer line; the design is similar to the drawing on this page.

Courtesy Railway World

The 10 mile section between Holt and Cromer was ready for opening by the following May, and on 23rd May, 1887 the Board of Trade was officially notified that the extension to Cromer was 'sufficiently complete for the safe carriage of passengers'. The BoT replied immediately, and the Eastern & Midlands Directors were told that Major General Hutchinson would inspect the works in June. Anticipating that the BoT inspector would 'pass' their new branch for passenger traffic, the Eastern & Midlands Directors announced that the line would be ready for opening in June; they had already decided that the E&MR terminus at Cromer would be known as 'Cromer Beach' to distinguish it from the rival Great Eastern Railway station on the far side of the town.

The prospect of a new rail link to and from Cromer was not universally welcomed by local people – many of whom no doubt felt that the existing GER line from Cromer to Norwich was adequate in relation to their transport needs. Indeed, at least one north Norfolk resident was positively opposed to the Eastern & Midlands line; a Mr Holding, who lived in the Weybourne area, claimed that the new railway ran too close to the main road between Cromer and Holt. This gentlemen felt so strongly about the nuisance that would thereby be created that he wrote a letter of complaint to the Board of Trade. Mr Holding's opposition may have been based upon a genuine fear that horses could easily be startled by the sudden appearance of noisy trains, or he may simply have disliked the railway on what would today be termed 'environmental grounds'. Whatever the reason, an isolated complaint was unlikely to impede the successful opening of the branch – however, matters took a more serious turn when Lt Ellis, RN, also complained to the Board of Trade.

Lieutenant Ellis argued that the new line was 'very close to the High Road between Weybourne and Sheringham', and accidents would (he thought) arise. His letter to the Board of Trade was tactfully-worded, and one senses that the lieutenant's concern was genuine; he 'ventured to suggest' that the railway company might introduce a system of signalling for road traffic 'whereby travellers on the High Road would be informed of the expected approach of a train'.

In fact, the railway did not impinge on the highway in an unacceptable way, the proximity of road and rail being no greater than usual in such situations. In this sense the lieutenant's ideas verged on eccentricity – but he happened to be an Inspecting Officer of Coast Guards and this may have added extra weight to an argument that could otherwise have been dismissed out of hand. The Board of Trade certainly took at least passing notice of Messrs Holding and Ellis, and Major General Hutchinson was asked to investigate the matter when he inspected the line in the following June.

Major General Hutchinson traversed the Holt to Cromer line at the beginning of June 1887, and one can well imagine the scene as the BoT Inspector's special passed slowly along the brand new railway. Leaving the existing 'terminus' at Holt, the special would have proceeded at little more than a walking pace, with frequent pauses as the Inspector stopped to examine the various new bridges and earthworks.

The Board of Trade Report

Having inspected the 10 mile line from end to end, Major General Hutchinson produced an extensive report; writing quickly in an untidy, difficult-to-read hand, the Inspector provided a valuable first-hand account of the Cromer extension,[3] and parts of his report may be worth quoting at length. The report, dated 4th June, 1887, started in the usual way, with an elegant introduction, followed by an outline summary of the works:

> Sir,
> I have the honour to report, for the information of the Board of Trade, that in compliance with the instructions contained in your minute of the 25th ult., I have inspected the extension of the Cromer branch of the Eastern & Midlands Railway from Holt to Cromer, a length of 10 miles 12 chains.
> The line is single, on the 4 ft 8½ inch gauge, the minimum width of formation level 16 ft, and the space between the lines, where there is more than one, 6 ft. Land has been purchased, and the overbridges constructed with a view to the future doubling of the line. The permanent way is . . . in good order.

The report then listed the over and underbridges *en route* to Cromer, with particular emphasis on the way in which they had been constructed. There were 'ten overbridges all constructed with brickwork, or concrete faced with brickwork abutments and piers'; the largest overbridge had a clear span of 24 ft. There were, in addition, 'six underbridges all built with brickwork abutments and piers' – two of these had brick arches, while the remaining four consisted of cast iron girders resting on brick piers; these were suitably strengthened with 'steel cross girders', and all of the works appeared to be 'substantially constructed and . . . standing well'. There were, continued the inspector:

> Several deep cuttings and high banks, the sides of which appear to be standing well. There are no tunnels. There are two level crossings of public roads, one at Holt and the other at Sheringham station, provided with gates. The crossing at 7 miles 43 chains described as . . . a public road is not so, but has merely been constructed in pursuance of the Act of 1881, which required the Company to provide a crossing between the two parts of Kelling Heath . . . the crossing is provided with proper gates and a lodge.
> The fencing is principally of post and wire with some short lengths of post and rail fence.
> The new stations are Sheringham and Cromer Beach, at both of which the necessary accommodation has been provided. Cromer Beach has been constructed as a large terminal station with extensive sidings. The signal arrangements are carried out in raised cabins at Sheringham and Cromer Beach, the former containing 12 working and 2 spare levers and the latter 18 working and 2 spare levers. The interlocking in these cabins is correct. An engine turntable has been constructed at Cromer.

In general, the Major General was pleased with the quality and stability of the new works, but he identified one or two minor deficiencies that would have to be rectified before the railway was opened. At Sheringham station, for instance, he pointed out that the clock 'should be placed so as to be visible from the platform', while 'huts' were needed 'at the two public level crossings'.

Interestingly, a simple platform had been erected at West Runton (possibly for ticket collection purposes) but the inspector warned that this facility 'should not be used . . . unless provided with proper signals'. There had also been considerable 'vertical or horizontal deviations' (to satisfy the demands of various local landowners); these unauthorised deviations did not, however, create any problems 'from an engineering point of view'.

Major General Hutchinson was particularly concerned about the complaints made to the Board of Trade by Lt Ellis and Mr Holding, and he had evidently considered the possibility that horses might be startled by passing trains:

> With regard to the two complaints from Lt. Ellis RN and Mr Holding as to the danger likely to arise to the vehicular traffic from the proximity of the railway to part of the road between Weybourne and Sheringham. I find that a screen has been erected along that part of the line to which the road most nearly approaches, and where the nature of the line allows. In addition to this, the Sheringham station down signals can be seen from the road when driving towards Sheringham, and I have suggested to the engineer whether the up starting signal cannot be raised so as to make it visible from the road for a considerable distance . . . I do not see what more can reasonably be done in the interests of the public using the highway in question.

The report concluded as follows:

> It is intended that the single line shall be worked on the train staff system and the necessary instruments have been provided. An undertaking so to work the single line is to be forwarded.
>
> Subject to the above named regulations, and to the receipt of the undertaking as to the mode of working, I see no objection to the Board of Trade authorising the line between Sheringham and Cromer being open to passenger traffic.

> I have, etc.,
> C.S. Hutchinson,
> Major General, R.E.

Board of Trade sanction having been obtained, the Cromer extension was opened on 16th June, 1887 – in good time for the summer tourist season which was expected to bring significant traffic to the new branch; the line from Holt had been completed in around 18 months at a cost of just £10,000 per mile.

Some Details of the Line

The completed line was, in many ways, a typical late-Victorian railway. Built at a relatively late date, it lacked architectural pretentions, and the intermediate stations were, for the most part, functional rather than flamboyant. There were, for example, no palatial waiting rooms or ornate bridges – the new line was built at a time when people accepted railways as a natural feature of the English landscape, and the promoters of the scheme saw no reason to disguise their new works as Medieval castles or Italianate villas. Neither was the line over-engineered, and although it featured some substantial earthworks at Cromer and elsewhere the chosen route followed the contours of the land as much as possible. As a result, the newly-opened railway incorporated numerous curves and several significant gradients – the steepest of which included stretches of 1 in 80 near Melton Constable and at Weybourne.

Only, perhaps, at Cromer did the line exhibit elements of modest grandeur, and here, where the new terminus was in open competition with the Great Eastern Railway, the line from Melton Constable ended in a large Tudoresque station with an overall roof spanning the central part of the platform. Yet, even at Cromer, only one main platform was provided, and the track layout was far from complex. In truth, Cromer Beach station was little more than a branch terminus at the end of a circuitous single line – though it was anticipated that the station would regularly handle large numbers of summer holidaymakers.

The Railway Engineer was certainly impressed by the new Cromer station, and in a brief, but very favourable report, this specialist engineering journal suggested that the Eastern & Midlands Railway had 'succeeded in erecting a very picturesque building without sacrificing in the least the accommodation necessary at a station which is extensively used by excursionists'. The new terminus was designed by William Marriott – though it is possible that local building contractors may also have been given an active role during the construction of the station (plans published by The Railway Engineer in January 1890 were, however, based upon originals supplied by Mr Marriott).

At Melton Constable the junction faced north-westwards rather than north-east towards Cromer – this configuration being a legacy of the original plan to serve Blakeney. Unfortunately, this arrangement did not permit direct running from London (or the Midlands) to Cromer and all through workings to or from Cromer would, of necessity, have to reverse in Melton Constable station prior to entering the branch. On the other hand, it was possible for local services from Norwich to continue northwards onto the Cromer line without reversal, and there would, in the years to come, be a limited amount of through running between the Norwich City and Cromer Beach branches.

As originally constructed the Melton to Cromer branch had just two intermediate stopping places at Holt and Sheringham, and of these the station at Holt was little more than an open platform. The simple platform at West Runton was brought into use in September 1887 and there were, thereafter, three small stations between Melton Constable and Cromer Beach. The original temporary station at Holt was soon rebuilt in more durable materials and – as we shall see – a further station was later opened at Weybourne, between Holt and Sheringham.

The new branch was, as expected, a welcome addition to the Eastern & Midlands network. The line had been opened in time for the summer tourist season, and it immediately contributed to Eastern & Midlands receipts, E&MR passenger figures for the 12 months ending 31st December, 1887 being 413,277 – an increase of 96,953 which, as the delighted E&MR Directors pointed out, was attributable chiefly to the traffic brought over their system by the recently-opened branch.

Abandonment of the Blakeney Scheme

The Cromer branch was of particular significance to the Eastern & Midlands Railway, and its completion in 1887 marked the high point of E & MR ambitions. There were, at this time, still lingering hopes that a branch to Blakeney Harbour might be constructed, but having at last reached Cromer the Eastern & Midlands Directors were reluctant to spend further money on the Blakeney scheme, and on 28th June, 1888 the Eastern & Midlands Railway obtained Powers to abandon the authorised line from Kelling to Blakeney. On a footnote, it may be worth adding that Lynn & Fakenham ticket stock books contained pages headed with the names of stations proposed for the Blakeney branch, and it is interesting to discover that, in addition to Blakeney itself, there would have been stations at Cley, Salthouse and Kelling.

While mentioning the abortive Blakeney branch, one might add that there were also suggestions that Blakeney and Cley-next-the-Sea could be served by a lightly-constructed tramway, but nothing came of this novel proposal. If implemented, the tramway scheme would have followed a slightly different route to that proposed in the 1880 Act, and whereas the line authorised in 1880 would have run north-westwards from its junction at Kelling, the later tramway route was to have diverged westwards from the Cromer line near Sheringham station and then continued due west along the remote north Norfolk coast via Weybourne, Salthouse, Cley-next-the-Sea and Blakeney. The line, which would have been worked as a light railway, would have served a remote, yet attractive coastal area that could have been developed for holiday traffic once the railway as in operation.

The Blakeney scheme was revived at the turn-of-the-century, and a possible light railway route was surveyed in 1901. Again, nothing tangible came of the proposal – though a station was eventually constructed at Weybourne, and this facility did much to fulfil the transport needs of people in the Weybourne and Salthouse areas.

Formation of the Midland & Great Northern Joint Committee

The Eastern & Midlands system was not in itself a particularly viable concern, but it nevertheless furnished the Midland and Great Northern companies with a useful outlet to the east coast. Holiday traffic was of particular importance by the 1890s, and railways were already playing a vital part in the exploitation of holiday regions such as Devon and Cornwall. Some lines (notably the Great Western) were well-placed to cater for this growing leisure traffic, though others were more or less land-locked. The Midland, for example, was solidly based in the central parts of England, and only at Morecambe did the MR touch the coast with a line of its own. The company was understandably keen to foster *all* kinds of traffic, and in terms of seaside traffic the Eastern & Midlands Railway presented a superb opportunity for further development. In 1889 the Midland obtained consent for a line from Saxby to Bourne, and when opened in 1894 this important 'cut-off' placed the Eastern & Midlands system in direct contact with populous East Midlands cities such as Leicester and Nottingham.

The Great Northern Railway was also actively involved with the Eastern & Midlands system, and although the E & MR remained nominally independent, it was clear to all concerned that the future of the line would ultimately rest in Great Northern or Midland hands.

The Midland was particularly keen to consolidate its role in Eastern & Midlands affairs for, as explained above, the E & MR gave the MR access to Sheringham, Cromer and a variety of other potentially-lucrative seaside resorts. Given that the Eastern & Midlands Railway lacked the resources to develop fully its bourgeoning system, the logic of the situation dictated that the Midland and GNR companies should play an even greater role in E & MR affairs and on 9th June, 1893 a new organisation known (appropriately enough) as 'The Midland & Great Northern Joint Committee' was formally created by Act of Parliament. A few days later, on 1st July, 1893, the Eastern & Midlands Railway was formally vested in the newly-formed M & GNJRC.

The Midland & Great Northern Joint Railway thereby assumed control of the Eastern & Midlands system, all E & MR rolling stock, surplus land and equipment being purchased for the sum of £160,000, while Eastern & Midlands shareholders received guaranteed dividends.

In theory, the Eastern & Midlands Railway simply passed into Midland and Great Northern ownership, but in practice the newly-created M & GNJR retained a large measure of autonomy, and the Midland & Great Northern exhibited most of the attributes of an independent concern, with its own locomotives, rolling stock, staff, insignia and management structure. The situation was similar to that pertaining in the case of the Somerset & Dorset Joint Railway (established 1875) or the Midland Railway Northern Counties Committee (created 1903); in each case, the railways concerned enjoyed virtual independence while having access to the immeasureably greater resources of the Derby-based company (the one obvious sign of Midland involvement being in terms of locomotive policy).

A New Station and Other Improvements

The M & GN lost no time in initiating a series of improvements throughout the former Eastern & Midlands system, the Cromer branch being one of the lines to benefit from these improvements. At Sheringham, for instance, the M & GN started work on an entirely new up side station building, and when this work was completed in 1897 the original waiting shelter was transferred to Eye Green (on the Peterborough Wisbech & Sutton Bridge section).

At the same time, the Midland & Great Northern Joint Committee started relaying the former Eastern & Midlands system with heavier-pattern 85 lb. per yard bullhead rail resting on conventional chaired sleepers; the line had originally been laid with 70 lb. per yard flat-bottomed contractor's rail – an adequate system, but one generally regarded as inferior in late Victorian England. The new trackwork was soon installed on the main running lines, but older flat-bottomed rail remained in situ in Cromer Beach goods yard and in other out-of-the-way parts of the system (Edwardian photographs clearly show the two types of trackwork in use at the same time, the 70 lb. per yard contractor's rail being noticeably smaller than the M & GN chaired variety).

Another improvement put into effect under M&GN auspices concerned the way in which the predominantly single track Midland & Great Northern network was signalled. When opened, the Cromer Beach line (and other parts of the system) had been worked on the train-staff-and-ticket system, whereby a series of trains in an up or down sequence could enter single line sections after the drivers had been given written authorisation in lieu of the single line staff; the staff itself would then be taken to the opposite end of the section by the last train in a series. This method of single line operation worked well enough, but it was decided that the more modern electric tablet system would be introduced, one of the lines to be so equipped being the Melton Constable to Cromer route, which received its new signalling equipment during the 1890s.

Further changes were put into effect in 1900 when the M&GN decided that a new stopping place would be built near Weybourne. As we have seen, there had been extraordinary vacillation about the Blakeney line, and the decision to erect a new station between Holt and Sheringham may have been prompted, at least in part, by a desire to serve an area that had not hitherto enjoyed the advantages of a rail link. Accordingly, on 6th September, 1900, the M&GN informed the Board of Trade that an additional station was to be built 'in the tablet section between Holt and Sheringham'.

Weybourne station was 'nearing completion' by June 1901, and at the end of that month this new facility was inspected by Major Druitt of the Board of Trade. As usual, the BoT Inspector produced a full report[4] with much interesting information about the brand new station:

28th June 1901

Sir,
    I have the honour to report for the information of the Board of Trade that in compliance with the instructions contained in your minute of the 15th June, I have inspected the new station at Weybourne on the Cromer branch of the Midland & Great Northern Joint Line.
    Weybourne station forms a new passing place and block post and tablet station on the single line from Melton to Cromer, and is situated between Holt and Sheringham stations.
    A new loop has been laid 400 yards in length for the passenger platform lines, and both the up and down platforms are 350 feet long, 12 feet wide and 3 feet 6 inches above rail level.
    On the down platform, station buildings have been erected with the booking office and general waiting room . . . a ladies waiting room and conveniences for both sexes. Also a station master's office and waiting room.
    On the up platform a shelter has been erected, which is sufficient for the present traffic at the station.
    Two sidings with a horse and carriage dock and cattle pen have been laid in on the down side . . . the bridge carrying the public road over the line near the station has been rebuilt.
    The signal cabin and frame, which are both new, contain 16 working and 4 spare levers, and the interlocking is correct. At the west side of the new loop, the bridge over the stream known as Weybourne Spring has been widened to allow a second line to be laid over it. It consists of a single span brick arch of 30 feet, and has ample theoretical strength. It appears to be well constructed and to be standing well.

No foot overbridge or separate access has been provided to the up platform, and passengers have to cross the line to get to the up trains. As the passenger traffic will, for the present at any rate, be small, I think this may be accepted.

All arrangements being satisfactory, I can recommend the Board of Trade to sanction the use of the new station at Weybourne.

I have, etc.,

F. Druitt,

Major, R.E.

Maps prepared in connection with the inspection show that the new station was fully signalled with up and down home, starting and distant signals, and there were also several ground discs. The provision of an additional crossing loop at this point increased line capacity on the Cromer route and also broke up the 6¼ mile block section between Holt and Sheringham into two smaller sections, that between Holt and Weybourne being 3½ miles long while the Weybourne–Sheringham section was 2¾ miles long.

On a footnote, it is interesting to discover that Weybourne signal box was originally to have been sited at the eastern end of the up platform, but this position seems to have presented visibility problems in that the nearby road overbridge prevented an unobstructed view along the line towards Holt. The box was finally sited near the centre of the gently-curved platform so that signalmen could obtain a clear view in each direction; a single storey cabin was required in order to allow signalmen to see beneath the brick arch.

Motive Power in the Eastern & Midlands Era

When opened in 1879 the Lynn & Fakenham Railway was worked by two Hudswell, Clarke 4–4–0Ts, numbered 8 and 9 in the company's list, and named *Hillington* and *Fakenham* respectively. Other engines of this same general type were ordered later, while further examples were added when the Yarmouth & North Norfolk Railway was amalgamated with the Lynn & Fakenham.

Another class employed on the Eastern & Midlands system during the early days was a group of eight Sharp, Stewart 0–6–0 tanks that had been purchased second-hand from the Great Western Railway. Originally built for the Cornwall Minerals Railway, they had been designed to work in pairs, coupled back-to-back; in Eastern & Midlands service they carried the numbers 1, 2, 3, 11, 12, 13, 14 and 18; Nos. 1, 2 and 3 were named *Melton Constable*, *Reepham*, *Blakeney* respectively.

The Hudswell, Clarke 4–4–0Ts and ex-Cornwall Minerals engines were probably used on the Cromer line during the 19th century, and all of these locomotives would have been seen at Melton Constable at one time or another. Another locomotive used in the early years was former LNWR 2–4–0 No. 42; like the Cornwall Minerals 0–6–0s, this engine had an interesting history, having started life as Lancaster & Carlisle No. 1 *Rickerby*. Built by Rothwell & Co. in 1857, it was a typical Trevithick-Allan engine with 17 in. × 20 in. outside cylinders. The engine later became LNWR No. 377, and in 1881 it was sold to the Eastern & Midlands Railway, together with sister engine No. 384 (ex-L&CR No. 8 *Luck of Edenhall*). Both locomotives were rebuilt by the Eastern & Midlands Railway in 1891 and, as a result, they received built-up chimneys, motion and tender tanks. These veteran engines were placed on the duplicate list in 1894 and, nearing the end of their lives, they were relegated to local freight work; in this capacity No. 42 (42A after 1894) ended its days working the Cromer pick-up freight.

At the end of its independent existence the Lynn & Fakenham Railway ordered a series of Beyer, Peacock 4–4–0s, and these engines were delivered at intervals during the next few years. The first four arrived in Norfolk in March 1882, and they received the numbers 21, 22, 23 and 24; four additional engines were delivered in 1883 (after the formation of the Eastern & Midlands Railway). These new arrivals were given the consecutive numbers 25, 26, 27 and 28. Another batch of three engines joined the E&MR fleet in 1886, and the class was completed in 1888 when a final group of four Beyer, Peacock 4–4–0s entered service. The new engines were numbered in the same series as their sisters, the 1886 engines being Nos. 29, 30 and 31 while the 1888 batch took the numbers 32, 33, 34 and 35.

The fifteen-strong Beyer, Peacock class initiated the widespread use of 4–4–0s on the Eastern & Midlands/M&GN system; they had 6 ft coupled wheels and 3 ft bogie wheels, together with 17 in. × 24 in. outside cylinders. They were, in many ways, similar to the Beyer, Peacock 4–4–0s delivered to the London & South Western Railway in 1882, while somewhat similar engines (albeit with inside cylinders) were constructed by Beyer, Peacock for the Great Northern Railway of Ireland. Nos. 32–35 were ordered specifically to work the extra traffic generated by the opening of the Cromer line, but in practice all of the Beyer, Peacock 4–4–0s appeared on the branch. Photographic evidence reveals that Nos. 32–35 were used on the Melton to Cromer line during the 1880s and 1890s, while Nos. 25, 28 and 29 were among those seen on the line around 1920. In later years, the engines were reboilered with typical Midland-style boilers, but their outside cylinders were a distinctly non-Midland feature that underlined their Beyer, Peacock origins.

In Lynn & Fakenham days, engines had been painted in a green livery with black and white lines, and the first Beyer, Peacock 4–4–0s carried this colour scheme. Nos. 25–28, in contrast, sported a chocolate brown livery that became the standard E&MR colour scheme; lining was said to have been black and chrome yellow and – despite the financial difficulties that plagued the poverty-stricken Eastern & Midlands Railway – the engines were always well turned-out, with burnished metalwork and gleaming paint!

There can be no doubt that, whatever financial considerations may have impinged upon the E&MR Company, its trains must have made a fine sight as they laboured up and down the hilly Cromer line on their way to the sea.

An early view of the station buildings at Melton Constable, showing a range of typical Marriott-designed structures.

Chapter Three
A Seaside Branch Line (1901–1918)

The decision to build a line from Melton Constable to Cromer rather than one to Blakeney was, in retrospect, an eminently sensible one, for although the tiny port of Blakeney would no doubt have benefited from a new railway, it could never have rivalled Cromer as a source of traffic for the Midland & Great Northern system.

Through Services from London

As mentioned in Chapter One, the opening of the line from Melton coincided with the start of the 'Poppyland' era, and by the turn-of-the-century large numbers of people were eager to visit,

> The land of the poppies . . . the home of the corn,
> And the cliffs of fern, where from night to morn,
> There is nothing but rest and a welcome peace,
> Where the weary voices of children cease,
> And the stars shine out and the sun dies down,
> To light a path to Cromer Town.

The lure of Clement Scott's famed 'Poppyland' was such that Cromer attracted large numbers of summer visitors throughout the late Victorian and early twentieth century periods. Many of these visitors travelled via the Great Eastern route from Liverpool Street, but in the hope that London residents might be tempted to sample the rival Eastern & Midlands route the E & MR collaborated with the GNR in the provision of through Kings Cross to Cromer expresses. Indeed, through services from London were a feature of the Melton to Cromer line from its very inception, the first Kings Cross to Cromer service being provided in August 1887 – initially on a summer-only basis.

There were two fast services from London by 1888, with departures from Kings Cross at 10.10 am and 2.00 pm. The 2.00 pm slipped a coach at Peterborough, and this was taken on to Melton, Holt, Sheringham and Cromer, giving an overall journey time of 4½ hours. All-year-round through services were introduced in 1891, and in 1894 the GNR started running its own 'Cromer Express' in open competition with the Great Eastern Railway's prestige express services from Liverpool Street; the Great Northern train left Kings Cross at 3.00 pm, this time being adhered to for many years.

In 1906 the 3.00 pm from Kings Cross reached South Lynn in 158 minutes and arrived in Cromer by 7.14 pm, its journey time from London being 4½ hours. A return service left Cromer Beach at 12.20 pm, and after a non-stop run from Peterborough to Finsbury Park it reached Kings Cross by 5.15 pm. There was also, for a short period around 1897, a fast summer-only express from Kings Cross to Cromer at 1.10 pm, and this very commendable working reached Cromer Beach in only 3¾ hours, with stops at Finsbury Park, Peterborough, Melton Constable and Sheringham; similar timings were adhered to in the up direction. Later, however, this service was decelerated, and in 1901 the down train took 4 hours 5 minutes – though the corresponding up service accomplished its journey in 3 hours 50 minutes. In 1909 the service was altered to provide a fast journey time to and from Scarborough,

Cromer being served by through coaches that were detached at Peterborough and reached the Norfolk coast resort in a little under 4 hours.

The GNR–M&GN route from Cromer to London via Melton Constable and Peterborough had its devotees, but the route was never as popular as the rival GER line. In retrospect, the popularity of the Great Eastern route was perhaps inevitable; after all, the Great Eastern had a more direct route, and its best trains were able to cover the intervening 138 miles in under 3 hours. One possible objection to the GER route concerned the Great Eastern terminus at Liverpool Street, which was poorly-sited in relation to London's best residential districts. However, even this minor problem was circumvented by the provision of GER through portions between Cromer (GER) and St Pancras which were detached at Ely, giving travellers a choice of routes to either St Pancras or Liverpool Street – the former terminus being better-placed in relation to fashionable areas of Victorian London such as Highgate and Hampstead. At a time when many of Cromer's patrons were drawn from the ranks of the upper middle classes, the option of travelling to and from St Pancras via the GER was of immense value, and in these circumstances it is clear that few London travellers would have used the M&GN route when the Great Eastern system offered a far better alternative.

A point which should be made here is that until the widespread introduction of holidays with pay, seaside towns such as Cromer were *residential* towns rather than holiday centres, and it follows that daily commuter traffic was as at least as important as purely holiday traffic. Those who travelled to and from Cromer were often residents for all or part of the year, and for this reason the Great Eastern Railway specialised in the provision of fast morning up and evening down trains in order that businessmen or professional people could be at their London offices in reasonable time. It is true that the celebrated 'Norfolk Coast Express' was intended to convey holidaymakers *to* Cromer, but this famous working ran only in the summer months, whereas the heavily-loaded morning up and evening down business expresses operated throughout the year (see *The Cromer Branch* (Oakwood Press) for further details of the GER line).

M&GN Through Services from Leicester & Birmingham

The Midland & Great Northern system was unable to compete effectively for London business traffic but it was, on the other hand, well-able to carry travellers to and from East Midlands cities such as Leicester and Nottingham. Although not as wealthy or populous as London, these Midland cities were both rising and prosperous manufacturing centres. Leicester, for example, had grown from a country town of 17,000 people in 1800 to a bustling city with a population of 154,000 by the early 1890s; at the end of the 19th century its population had reached 219,000. With an economy based firmly upon hosiery and related industries, Leicester had a prosperous middle class, many of whom chose to spend their summers by the sea, and 'Poppy-land' (being linked to Leicester by the Midland & Great Northern Railway) was an obvious venue for these well-off holidaymakers. It comes as no surprise to discover that, from the time of its opening, the M&GN Cromer branch catered for Leicester traffic; in 1887, for instance, a through train was run between Cromer Beach and Peterborough, and this working enabled Leicester passengers to reach their destination by changing at South Lynn or at Peterborough (from where the London & North Western Railway provided a useful link to Leicester).

Through services from Cromer to Leicester via the direct Bourne to Saxby line had been introduced in 1897. These services – which conveyed Yarmouth, Norwich and Cromer portions and were sometimes hauled by M & GN engines throughout – enabled through travellers to reach Leicester in 3¾ hours, typical timings being as shown below:

UP		DOWN	
Cromer Beach	dep. 9.50 am	Leicester	dep. 2.45 pm
Melton	dep. 10.28 am	Melton	dep. 5.39 pm
Leicester	arr. 1.13 pm	Cromer Beach	arr. 6.15 pm

As an added bonus, the through Cromer to Leicester trains ran to and from Birmingham, although Leicester was probably a more important source of Cromer holiday traffic. Until 1902, the through Leicester services ran only during the summer months, but thereafter the service was maintained on an all-year-round basis.

The volume of traffic between Leicester and Cromer was much less than that conveyed by the Great Eastern route to London at the turn-of-the-century, and it is impossible to estimate how many East Midlands businessmen migrated to Sheringham or Cromer during the summer. It is conceivable that some individuals may have sent their families to Cromer for the duration of the school holidays, and then used the railway to visit them at weekends, while some businessmen may have travelled between Cromer and Leicester on a semi-regular basis. Whatever arrangements were made, there is no doubt that the existence of the M & GN fostered a special relationship between East Midlands cities such as Leicester, and Norfolk resorts such as Cromer and Great Yarmouth. These links became established during the late-Victorian period when middle class holidaymakers 'discovered' Cromer, while, in later years, ordinary working class families also discovered the delights of Cromer – and when holidays with pay became a recognised feature of British life the links between Cromer and the East Midlands were further consolidated.

Excursions and Local Traffic

Annual two-week summer holidays were not a feature of Victorian or Edwardian life, and as we have seen, the vast majority of Cromer's patrons were of middle or upper class origins – many of whom actually resided in the town. Day trips were, on the other hand, a Victorian institution, and at a time of slowly rising living standards the M & GN and GER railways both realised that there was a vast, untapped market in terms of working class leisure travel. It was, indeed, in the field of cheap day tickets that the Midland & Great Northern and GER companies competed most vigorously, and on Sundays or Bank Holidays (i.e. when normal traffic was slack) it was usually possible to reach Cromer from either Kings Cross or the GER station at Liverpool Street. In 1903, for example, the Great Northern offered a day return ticket from London to Cromer or Great Yarmouth for only 4 shillings, while Sunday afternoon half day excursions from Norwich (or other local towns) became a regular 'treat' for local Sunday school children. In the opposite direction, the M&GN ran day excursions to destinations as varied as Nottingham, Matlock and Aberystwyth!

The annual 'Wakes Week' holidays in Northern industrial towns gave rise to additional through excursion trains over the M&GN routes to Cromer and Great Yarmouth, while at the other end of the social scale the Midland & Great Northern was able to develop a flourishing traffic in golfers. In this context it is important to remember that there were a number of first class golf courses in the Cromer area – among them the 18-hole Royal Cromer Golf Club's course near the lighthouse at Cromer. There was another golf course beside the M&GN line at Sheringham, and at a time when golfing holidays were becoming increasingly popular among the middle classes, the Midland & Great Northern offered special golfers' season tickets as a means of encouragement for potential golf-playing travellers!

The Cromer branch provided local residents (and summer visitors) with a useful choice of through trains to London and the Midlands, while ordinary branch services consisted of around a dozen trains in each direction. In July 1908 there were 13 up and 13 down workings, including the 12.45 and 3.20 pm through services to Kings Cross and the 9.50 am departure for Leicester and Birmingham.

Other services left Cromer Beach at 8.00, 8.55, 10.40, 11.45 am, 1.40, 2.00, 5.25, 6.18, 7.23 and 8.15 pm. Some of these workings continued beyond Melton Constable to reach Peterborough or other destinations, and there appear to have been a number of through trips to Norwich City (though careful study of the timings suggests that most local trains reversed at Melton Constable). Average journey times, for the 15 mile trip between Cromer and Melton Constable, were about 32–39 minutes, the up services being marginally faster than those in the down direction. In the reverse direction, balancing down workings left Melton Constable at 8.35, 9.43, 10.40 am, 12.20, 1.16, 2.17, 2.55, 3.22, 3.55, 4.18, 6.06, 6.35, and 8.12 pm. In general, trains called at all of the intermediate stations between Melton and Cromer Beach, but the London and Leicester expresses called at Weybourne only to set down.

A similar situation pertained in the up direction, in that the 9.50 am 'Leicester' called at Weybourne to pick-up only, while the 12.45 London express missed out this station altogether. Curiously, the 12.45 pm did call at West Runton, albeit to pick-up only, and the 9.50 am Leicester express also called to pick-up at this tiny, halt-like stopping place. Some early evening trains called at Weybourne only by request, and intending passengers were expected to inform the guard of their intention to alight (or give a hand signal to the driver if they wanted to be picked-up). These restrictions did not apply to West Runton which – in the summertime at least – benefited from its proximity to the coast and was consequently used by walkers, golfers and other holidaymakers.

The 2.00 pm up service from Cromer to Melton and beyond conveyed a through portion for Manchester, and for this reason the service was treated as an express. It called at West Runton to pick-up 'for Peterborough and beyond', and omitted Weybourne altogether; at Melton Constable it combined with through portions from Norwich and Great Yarmouth, and went forward from Melton at 2.50. Sunday services were provided during the summer months, and the July 1908 timetable shows that there were three up and three down trains between Cromer and Melton, with a short distance working in the up direction between Cromer Beach and Sheringham.

The Mundesley-on-Sea Branch

The Great Eastern Railway had initially viewed the M&GN as an intruder in Norfolk, but although the the two organisations still regarded each other with suspicion they soon realised the advantages of co-operation, and in 1898 the Midland & Great Northern joined forces with the Great Eastern to form the Norfolk & Suffolk Joint Committee. The committee immediately assumed responsibility for a short branch from North Walsham to Mundesley-on-Sea; this line had originated in 1888 as an Eastern & Midlands venture, but little was done until the formation of the M&GN. In its original form, the Mundesley line was a short, dead-end branch, but in 1896 the Midland obtained Parliamentary consent for a continuation of the line beyond its existing terminus to Cromer. This new line would be jointly-owned, and it was hoped that, once in operation, the new route would stimulate resort development in the picturesque Overstrand era – the very heart of Clement Scott's much-publicised 'Poppyland'.

The projected Cromer to Mundesley line was, in essence, an extension of the existing branch from Melton Constable, but as Cromer Beach station was situated in a built-up area the new route would join the Melton line by means of a triangular junction between Cromer Beach and West Runton stations. The land needed for the proposed line was purchased by 1902, and construction was under way in the early part of the following year; a few months later, in September 1904, it was reported that the major earthworks between Mundesley and Cromer were well advanced, though the junctions at Cromer had 'not yet been commenced'.

Work continued throughout the next few months, some problems being experienced with local landowners who were antipathetic towards the new line; William Marriott who, as M&GN Engineer, was actively involved in the Mundesley scheme, recalled that the railway-builders were 'badly hit by the high prices' asked for some of the land.[5]

Eventually, in July–August 1906, the jointly-owned route from Mundesley to Cromer was opened for public traffic. Approaching Cromer from the east, the new line tunnelled beneath the Great Eastern station to reach its junction with the GER at Roughton Road.* Westwards, the route continued to Newstead Lane Junction, at which point the line forked, with one line running north-westwards to join the Melton to Cromer branch at Runton West Junction while the other arm diverged north-eastwards to converge with the branch at Runton East Junction. A brief report of the opening

*See map on page 6.

appeared in the September 1906 edition of the *Locomotive Magazine*, which noted that:

> The new Sheringham line, branching from the Norwich to Cromer section and converging with the N&SJt Railway at Roughton Road Junction and thence via Newstead Lane Junction to Runton West Junction on the Sheringham and Cromer Beach line of the Midland & Great Northern Joint, was opened on July 23rd with GER engine No. 678 . . . the new coast line from Mundesley via Trimingham and Overstrand to Roughton Road Junction, there forming part of the GER new Sheringham route, was opened on August 3rd. Two spur lines from Newstead Lane Junction, the next junction after Roughton Road Junction, give access respectively to Runton West Junction, West Runton and Sheringham, and to Runton East Junction and Cromer Beach, on the Midland and Great Northern Joint Ry. The first GER train, Overstrand to North Walsham (GER) was worked by tank locomotive No. 591, and the first Joint Company's train, Mundesley to Cromer Beach, was worked by the Midland Ry tank locomotive No. 143.

The completed line enabled Great Eastern trains to reach Sheringham, while at the same time the Midland & Great Northern was furnished with an alternative, albeit circuitous path for trains running between North Walsham and Melton Constable. The line was administered by the Norfolk & Suffolk Joint Committee, and the intermediate stations at Overstrand, Trimingham and Mundesley-on-Sea were provided with lavish passenger facilities to accommodate the heavy holiday traffic that was expected to materialise once the line became fully established. A fourth station was provided at Paston & Knapton, on the original North Walsham to Mundesley section, and this too was exceptionally well-built.

Mundesley-on-Sea and Paston stations had been erected by Messrs Cornish & Gaymer, while Overstrand and Trimingham were built by C.A. Sadler of Sheringham; Mundesley was said to have been 'one of the prettiest and best . . . for many miles around'. The principal engineering feature on the North Walsham–Mundesley–Cromer line was a five-span arched viaduct between Newstead Lane and Runton West junctions.

The line was, from its inception, worked by trains from both of the owning companies, the usual practice being for Great Eastern branch trains to run from North Walsham GER station to Mundesley or Overstrand, while Midland & Great Northern locals ran between Cromer Beach and Overstrand, Mundesley or North Walsham (M&GN). The Great Eastern also ran important express trains to and from Sheringham – where the M&GN station had been enlarged to handle the extra traffic. At Cromer Beach, meanwhile, Mundesley services ran to and from a bay platform on the south side of the station, and in view of the anticipated congestion in the Runton–Cromer area, the M&GN doubled the Cromer branch between Runton West Junction and Cromer Gas Works Siding; the line remained single track between the gas works siding and Cromer Beach station.

Curiously, the new joint line did not meet with universal approval. As mentioned above, there was considerable opposition from certain landowners in the Mundesley area, but this was, perhaps, to be expected from people who had chosen to live in North Norfolk because of its exclusive atmosphere and attractive coastal scenery. More surprisingly, the line was openly criticised by G.A. Sekon, the editor of the *Railway Magazine* who, in September 1904, had complained that the route was poorly planned, and indeed unnecessary:

> This new line of the Norfolk and Suffolk Joint Committee, from Mundesley to near Sheringham, offered an excellent opportunity to the Great Eastern Railway and the Joint Midland and Great Northern Railway to construct a central and commodious joint station in Cromer, but the opportunity was not taken advantage of, and the new line makes a considerable detour, completely avoiding Cromer.
>
> So far as the Great Eastern Railway is concerned – whose object is to reach Sheringham – the course of the new line between Cromer and the junction with the Joint Midland and Great Northern Railway near West Runton is all that can be desired, but its course cannot be very satisfactory to the Joint Midland and Great Northern Railway, as Cromer Beach remains a terminal station, and when the new line is completed and through trains from Melton Constable, Mundesley, Yarmouth and Lowestoft are run over it, Cromer Beach will be a 'dead end', inconvenient to work and with awkward train connections. To minimise this inconvenience as much as possible it is proposed to work both up and down Midland and Great Northern trains into and out of Cromer Beach . . . but this method of working will mean an addition of about 3 miles to the train mileage of each train and quite ¼ hour will be added to the length of the journey to and from places eastward of Cromer.

According to Sekon, the railways concerned did 'not even pretend' that the new railway could ever be made to pay, its only *raison d'etre* being 'the desire of the competing companies to keep each other out of the district'. In other words (thought Sekon) the Cromer to Mundesley-on-Sea line was no more than an expensive charade, designed to prevent wasteful competition in an area that had, by 1900, become of great importance to both the M&GN and the GER. On the other hand, he felt that, by letting the Great Eastern have access to Sheringham, the Midland & Great Northern had caused itself real harm insofar as the M&GN dealt with 'more passengers at Sheringham than it did at Cromer'. At Cromer, the shorter route of the GER gave the latter company a distinct advantage, but at Sheringham the Midland & Great Northern had, hitherto, enjoyed a monopoly. Having allowed the GER into Sheringham the M&GN had opened the way for real competition between the two routes, and Sekon anticipated that the summer of 1907 would:

> . . . see fierce competition for the London–Sheringham traffic. The Joint Midland and Great Northern Railway's best train now takes 3 hours 38 minutes. The Great Eastern Railway's best to Cromer takes 2 hours 55 minutes, so that, assuming the train for Sheringham does not run into and out of Cromer station, the objective ought to be reached in 3 hours 10 minutes from Liverpool Street. Against this, Kings Cross is more convenient for a large number of the class of people who visit Sheringham than is Liverpool Street, so that the 28 minutes difference in the timing looks more on paper than it really counts for.

In retrospect, G.A. Sekon was probably correct in his view that the newly-built Norfolk & Suffolk Joint Line between North Walsham and Cromer was an unnecessary scheme that can have generated little originating traffic. Mundesley, Overstrand and neighbouring villages such as Sidestrand stubbornly refused to develop as major holiday resorts, and from the M&GN's point of view the money expended on this expensive route could well have been spent on better things. On the other hand, the N&SJ line provided a useful link between the M&GN and GER routes at Cromer, and in the longer term this link (which enabled the GER to reach Sheringham) was destined to be of great importance to the Cromer Beach line.

The opening of the Norfolk & Suffolk Joint line between Cromer, Mundesley and North Walsham enabled the M&GN and GER to operate a variety of through services over the new line, and both partners seized the opportunity to extend their prestige express services. The Great Eastern's crack train – the 'Cromer Express' was made into a (nominal) 12 coach formation with sections for Cromer, Overstrand and Sheringham, and in view of the diverse range of destinations now catered for the service was renamed 'The Norfolk Coast Express'. It was usual for the train to be divided at North Walsham, from where eight coaches were worked forward to Cromer (GER) while two vehicles were taken along the Norfolk & Suffolk Joint route to Mundesley and Overstrand; the remaining portion was worked through to Sheringham via Cromer Junction, Runton West Junction and the M&GN line.

Not to be outdone, the Midland & Great Northern extended its best London through services to Mundesley, the usual practice being for Mundesley portions to be worked on to Mundesley after reversal at Cromer Beach. It is possible that the 'Leicesters' also conveyed Mundesley portions (although Edwardian timetables do not make the position entirely clear).

Motive Power Notes

The Eastern & Midlands locomotive department passed into Midland control on the formation of the Midland & Great Northern Joint Committee, but William Marriott was allowed to remain in charge at Melton Constable and this ensured a degree of continuity between the old and the new regimes. There was, nonetheless, a pressing need for new motive power to work the M&GN system, and although the Beyer Peacock 4–4–0s were, by all accounts, excellent machines,'the first engines ordered by the Midland & Great Northern were standard Midland-style engines, built to S.W. Johnson's familiar Midland design. The first batch (Nos. 36, 37, 38, 39, 42, 43, 44, 45, 46, and 47) were built by Sharp, Stewart & Co, in 1894, and these were followed by 16 more from the same maker; the final seven were, in contrast, Beyer, Peacock products.

There were, in all, no less than 26 Johnson 4–4–0s on the M&GN, and these engines were, with the slightly earlier Beyer, Peacock locomotives, the type most usually seen on the Melton to Cromer branch in Midland & Great Northern days.

The Johnson 4–4–0s had 6 ft 6 in. coupled wheels and 3 ft 3 in. bogie wheels, together with 18 in. × 26 in. inside cylinders; they weighed 42 tons 10 cwt and had a boiler pressure of 160 psi. The engines were, collectively, known as class 'C', the older Beyer, Peacock engines becoming class 'A' under M&GN auspices.

It is interesting to reflect that the Midland Railway was involved in the running of three large subsidiary companies, two of which (the Somerset & Dorset and M&GN) were jointly-owned, while the third (the Northern Coun-

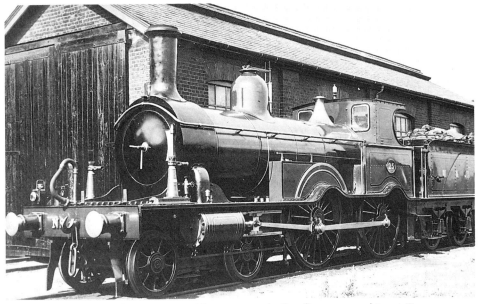

Beyer, Peacock class 'A' 4–4–0 No. 25 pauses in the afternoon sunshine at Cromer shed during the early 1900s. This engine was built in 1883 (Works No. 2338).

Loco. Publishing Co.

An early view of Johnson class 'C' 4–4–0 No. 36, seen here at Cromer Beach in the 1890's. Note the original style of 'Joint' lettering – JᵀM & GNR. *Loco. Publishing Co.*

ties Committee) was a wholly-owned subsidiary. In all three cases, Midland locomotive practices became prominent in various ways, but as a means of emphasising the separate identity of these subsidiaries, a distinctive locomotive livery was adopted in each case – S&DJR engines being blue while their Irish counterparts on the NCC were painted olive green. This theme was continued on the Midland & Great Northern, which, from 1893 onwards, started painting its engines in an attractive golden ochre livery with black and yellow lining and dark brown frames.

It is likely that all of the Johnson 4–4–0s appeared on the Cromer branch at one time or another, the through Cromer to Kings Cross workings being their star turn – although this prestige duty was also undertaken by the class 'A' 4–4–0s (which were said to be freer running). The 4–4–0s also worked freight duties, albeit on a sporadic basis. As a general rule, Cromer branch freight duties were handled by older, ex-E&MR engines or by standard Johnson 0–6–0 goods engines which, like the 'C' class 4–4–0s, resembled their sisters on the Midland proper. There were, in all, 16 Johnson 0–6–0s on the M&GN, these engines being known as class 'D'; they were numbered in sequence from 58 to 73 in the Midland & Great Northern locomotive fleet.

Midland engines appeared on the Cromer branch from time to time, and in 1906 three MR 0–4–4Ts were transferred to Norfolk in order to work the newly-opened Norfolk & Suffolk Joint line between Cromer and Mundesley-on-Sea. On 15th April, 1907 the *Locomotive Magazine* reported that:

> Three Midland Ry front coupled tank engines have been working in the Cromer district since the opening of the Mundesley and Cromer line. These engines still bear Midland Ry Nos. 142, 143 and 144, and retain the red painting, but the initials M&GN in brass letters have now been fixed on the tank sides.

The three Midland 0–4–4Ts remained on the M&GN for several years, and, in addition to their normal duties on the Norfolk & Suffolk Joint line they also appeared on the Melton to Cromer line. Overhaul and maintenance was undertaken at Melton Constable and the three engines were fitted with Whitaker tablet exchange apparatus so that they could be used on those parts of the M&GN system equipped with Whitaker tablet exchangers. Nos. 142, 143 and 144 were finally returned to the Midland Railway in 1912.

The use of these Midland locomotives added an element of variety that must have been welcomed by Edwardian railway enthusiasts, and in this context it is worth mentioning that Great Eastern engines also appeared regularly on the Cromer branch after 1906; the first GER passenger train into Sheringham was headed by Worsdell 'M15' class 2–4–2T No. 678, and thereafter these handsome 2–4–2Ts regularly worked over the section of line between Runton West Junction and Sheringham. Another 2–4–2T type seen on the GER Sheringham services was Holden's 5 ft 8 in. radial tanks which, like the 'M15s', often hauled Mundesley and Sheringham portions of the Great Eastern's crack expresses (these workings often ran via North Walsham, Mundesley and thence to Sheringham).

The most interesting tank locomotives employed on the M&GN Cromer branch were undoubtedly the three Melton-built 4–4–2Ts, Nos. 9, 20 and 41. These somewhat unusual 'Atlantic' tanks had been assembled in the

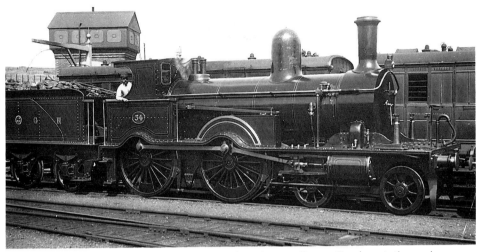

Beyer, Peacock 4–4–0 No. 34 stands in the sidings at Cromer Beach; note the rarely-photographed water tower on the left of the picture. *LCGB, Ken Nunn Collection*

Class 'C' 4–4–0 No. 53, poses for the camera outside Cromer Beach shed. Like their counterparts on the Midland Railway, these Johnson 4–4–0s were progressively rebuilt, a few with larger boilers, their boiler fittings being altered to fit the loading gauge. *Lens of Sutton*

M & GN's own workshops, and although they carried works plates claiming that they had been 'rebuilt Melton Constable' the three engines were in effect new machines. The first of the trio was No. 41, which emerged from the works in 1904, while Nos. 20 and 9 were completed in February 1909 and March 1910 respectively. The new engines had 6 ft coupled wheels and 17½ in. × 14 in. inside cylinders and their weight in working order was 68 tons 9 cwt. Most locomotive historians agree that the 4-4-2Ts incorporated a variety of spare parts, and perhaps for this reason their cylinders and motion resembled those provided on the class 'A' Beyer, Peacock 4-4-0s; Thomas Whitelegg of the London Tilbury & Southend Railway is said to have helped during the design stages of the engines.

The Atlantic tanks were used for many years on the Norfolk & Suffolk Joint lines between Yarmouth and Lowestoft, and North Walsham and Cromer, but they also worked on the Cromer to Melton Constable line – for which purpose one of them was stationed at Melton Constable and another at Cromer Beach. In later years their tanks were cut down (possibly for weight reasons), while in LNER days they were classified as class 'C17' and numbered 09, 020 and 041.

While on the subject of M & GN tank engines it would be appropriate to recall that the Melton Constable works shunter was known colloquially as 'Black Bess' on account of her LNWR-style lined black livery. The engine concerned had been built in 1877 as one of a pair of 0 6-0 saddle tanks ordered for service on the Great Yarmouth & Stalham Light Railway; these engines were constructed by Fox Walker & Co of Bristol, and later became E & MR Nos. 15 and 16. No. 16 (ex-*Stalham*) became Melton works shunter in 1901, and survived in that capacity until the demise of the works in 1936; the engine was well-looked after and could usually be seen lurking in some part of the labyrinthine interior of the works. A general summary of some of the locomotive types seen on the Melton Constable to Cromer Beach line is given in *Table 1* (*below*).

Table 1

CROMER BRANCH MOTIVE POWER c.1887 – 1923

Type	Wheelbase	Typical Numbers
Hudswell, Clarke	4-4-0T	9/10
Sharp, Stewart	0-6-0T	
Ex-LNWR	2-4-0	42
Beyer, Peacock class 'A'	4-4-0	23/25/28/29/31/32/33/34/35
Johnson class 'C'	4-4-0	1/3/17/18/36/39/51/53
Johnson class 'D'	0-6-0	
Marriott class 'A tank'	4-4-2T	9/20/41
Johnson Midland tank	0-4-4T	142/143/144
Worsdell 'M15' class*	2-4-2T	678

*GER engines used on through services to Sheringham.

The numbers shown in *Table 1* relate to engines known to have worked on the line at various times – the Midland 0–4–4Ts, for example, were recorded in the *Locomotive Magazine*, while the Beyer, Peacock class 'A' 4–4–0s were frequently photographed on the Cromer line. Conversely, the class 'C' 4–4–0s do not appear to have been photographed on the line on a regular basis, and on this (admittedly imperfect) evidence there would seem to be at least some justification for suggesting that the familiar class 'As' were the most characteristic locomotives on the Cromer branch in pre-grouping days.

Turning, briefly, to what might be termed 'less typical' types, there is evidence to suggest that Midland Railway locomotives reached Cromer Beach on several occasions. As we have seen, three Johnson 0–4–4Ts worked on the line on a regular basis, but in addition to these well-recorded visitors Kirtley 2–4–0s were not unknown on the branch, and there are photographs of Kirtley '800' class 2–4–0s at Cromer Beach. The engines concerned were (probably) on loan from the Midland – it is known that MR locomotives were hired to the M&GN during the 1890s (when the Joint Committee did not have enough modern engines to work the system).

World War One

On 4th August, 1914 the United Kingdom declared war on Imperial Germany after the Kaiser's armies had arrogantly marched into defenceless Belgium, and for the next four years East Anglia was in the front line of an expected German attack. On 3rd November, 1914 a squadron of German warships shelled Great Yarmouth, and although this raid was largely ineffective it gave substance to the theory that the enemy intended to launch some form of landing on the flat beaches of East Anglia. Norfolk and the other eastern counties were heavily garrisoned throughout the war – as early as 5th August, 1914 no less than 30 packed troop trains had brought men and equipment to Melton Constable and neighbouring Mundesley; Melton Constable became an armed camp with soldiers crammed into every available billet and barbed wire entanglements around the village and railway works!

Fortunately, no large scale German landing was ever attempted, and with the war bogged down on the Western Front the Germans used their terrifying new weapons – the Zeppelins – to bomb England from the air. Zeppelin raids took place at intervals throughout the war, the first raid being on 19th January, 1915 when Zeppelin 'L4' nosed its way inland to bomb Hunstanton and Kings Lynn.

It was soon realised that, in the absence of sophisticated navigational aids, airship commanders were using the railways as convenient navigational features, and despite the imposition of a nightly 'blackout', local railways such as the M&GN were involved in frequent Zeppelin incidents. On the night of 31st January/1st February, 1916, for example, Zeppelin No. L20 crossed the North Sea and, slipping inland at Sheringham, it then wandered aimlessly around the countryside before eventually dropping its load of high explosive bombs on Loughborough (the more important target of Leicester was missed because the city had been blacked-out as a precautionary measure).

In a later incident, Zeppelin No. L11 flew over north Norfolk and dropped an incendiary bomb near Wroxham[6] – fortunately with little effect. It remains a matter of conjecture why Zeppelin commanders should have acted as they did on some of these nocturnal raids, though one plausible explanation is that they were simply lost! Without the benefit of navigational aids, the airships were forced to rely on dead reckoning, chart reading and other traditional methods, and it is hardly surprising that railways such as the M&GN were used as landmarks.

Inevitably, the enemy aviators were drawn to Melton Constable (and other railway junctions) on a number of occasions. William Marriott recalled that, on one memorable night, the works received a telephone call from Aylsham to warn them that a 'Zepp' was heading for Melton Constable – and 'within five minutes she was overhead'. Sometimes the raids continued for two or three nights in a row, and it was perhaps fortunate that the M&GN had spent 'a large amount of money on roof blinds' for the workshops.

The works themselves were kept busy throughout the war, not only on routine work for the M&GN but also on a variety of war-related tasks. Over 30,000 shell noses, for example, were manufactured for the East Anglian Munitions Committee, while around 70 locomotives were repaired for the Midland Railway. (These engines were sometimes run-in on the Cromer or Norwich lines.)

Wartime train services were less frequent than those provided prior to 1914. The number of through trains to London was reduced to just one train each way, and the Leicester service was decelerated; in 1917 the London workings were withdrawn altogether.

Meanwhile, the M&GN and other railways were struggling to carry large numbers of servicemen to and from their posts in the threatened north Norfolk area. It was clear that, by 1917, the Germans were unlikely to invade England – but there was widespread fear of a hit-and-run raid (such as the British themselves launched against Zeebrugge on St George's Day, 1918). To guard against such an eventuality local railways such as the Melton to Cromer line were regularly patrolled by an armoured train, while as an added precaution, secret plans had earmarked certain stations as railheads to which troops could be despatched at immediate notice.

The armoured train was of particular interest. Built in the LNWR workshops at Crewe, it consisted of a heavily-armoured Great Northern Railway 'N2' class 0–6–2T marshalled between two bogie infantry vehicles (adapted from Great Western Railway 40 ton coal wagons) and two gun-carrying vehicles. The train was armed with maxim guns and naval-type 12-pounders, and it could be driven from either end, or in conventional fashion from the locomotive. This unusual unit spent much of its time on the Mundesley to Cromer line, with occasional forays along the branch to Melton Constable (or along neighbouring GER lines). The train was usually stationed at North Walsham, but maintenance was carried out in the M&GN workshops at Melton Constable.

In the event, fears of German attack were exaggerated, and the armoured train was never called upon to fire its guns in anger. Zeppelin raids nevertheless continued until the very end of the war, and on 19th October, 1917 no less than three of the raiders crossed the coast near Cromer. On other occasions, the hydrogen-filled airships were shot down in flames by naval aircraft stationed at RNAS aerodromes in the area – one of these air fields was at Holt.

The Great War finally ended on 11th November, 1918. The cost of ultimate victory had been very great, and the long lists of dead on town and village war memorials throughout the land remain to this day as mute reminders of those who made 'the supreme sacrifice' in the so-called 'War to End all Wars'.

Over 800 Midland & Great Northern railwaymen served in HM forces during the 1914–18 war, and over 100 died in the conflict. The victims included Second Lt Stanley Marriott – William Marriott's youngest son and a former employee at Melton Constable works (where he had studied under his father's expert tutelage). In his memoirs, the M&GN Manager relates how 'Driver English of Melton Constable' and two other Midland & Great Northern men went to find Second Lt Marriott's grave 'close to the road from Les-Boeufs to Miller's Daughter, where the windmill trench crosses the road'. They found the grave and sent William Marriott a sketch – refusing to accept any payment for their expenses; this touching anecdote illustrates, perhaps better than any other, the close 'family' relationships that grew up at Melton Constable works, and on the Midland & Great Northern generally.

In physical terms the war produced few obvious changes, though deferred maintenance and lack of regular cleaning must have had an adverse effect upon the appearance of the locomotives and rolling stock seen at Cromer Beach. The attractive M&GN yellow livery was retained for a few more years but, as time went by, some of the engines lost their bright yellow sheen and assumed a sort of light khaki hue. This eventually gave way to a dark brown colour, which eventually became the standard Midland & Great Northern livery for all engines.

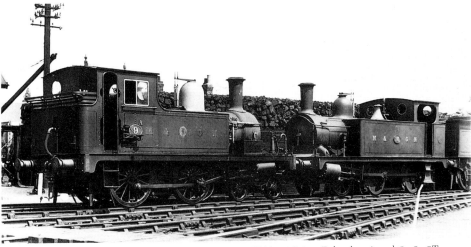

An interesting comparison of M&GN 4–4–0T No. 9A (ex *Fakenham*) and 0–6–0T No. 16. The 4–4–0 was a veteran of the Lynn & Fakenham Railway, while the 0–6–0T was built at Melton Constable in 1905, using parts of a former Cornwall Minerals locomotive. Photographed on 26th June, 1929.   *H.C. Casserley*

Class 'C' 4–4–0 No. 37 was still in more or less original condition when photographed by Mr Casserley at Melton Constable on 1st July, 1936. The extended smokebox was, however, fitted to all of the Johnson 4–4–0s.

H.C. Casserley

Built at Melton Constable works, diminutive 0–6–0T No. 99 was constructed in 1902 using many components from a withdrawn Black, Hawthorn saddle tank. The engine was re-numbered 099 by the LNER in 1936 and finally withdrawn in 1945. Lens of Sutton

Marriott 4–4–2T No. 20 makes a spirited start from Cromer Beach during the early 1930s. Cromer's curiously-proportioned water tower can clearlybe seen. Loco Publishing Co.

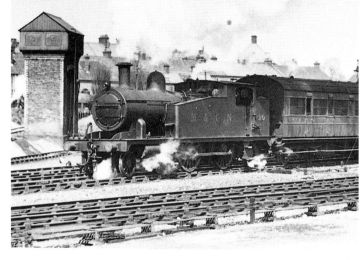

Class 'C' 4–4–0 No. 6 (as LNER No. 06) stands in the main platform at Cromer Beach on 14th March, 1939. *H.C. Casserley*

Class 'C' 4–4–0 No. 80 awaits its next turn of duty at Melton Constable in 1934; this engine was one of the Beyer, Peacock 'C' class that were built in 1899 (Nos. 74–80). *H.C. Casserley*

Two class 'C' 4-4-0s stand in the locomotive yard at Melton Constable in 1932. The nearer engine (No. 38) sports a cut-down chimney, whilst the other locomotive has acquired a Belpaire boiler, Deeley cab and other refinements.
Loco. Publishing Co.

Built at Melton Constable works in 1904, this Marriott 4-4-2T, No. 41, was frequently seen on the Cromer branch services.
Loco. Publishing Co.

Johnson class 'D' 0-6-0 No. 62 received a large boiler in 1906 and a Belpaire boiler in 1923, these rebuildings being carried out at Melton Constable works. This 1935 view shows the locomotive in its final form.   H.C. Casserley

Chapter Four

Twentieth Century Developments (1918–1948)

The end of the Great War in November 1918 was followed by a severe influenza epidemic that killed thousands of people, but the miseries of war finally came to an end and, in the summer of 1919, people flocked once more to the seaside. On the railways, the disruptions of the war years were slowly put back to normal – although the transition to normal conditions was marred by a damaging coal strike in 1921.

Branch Train Services in the 1920s

Post war train services were not as good as those provided during the Edwardian period, and although the through Kings Cross to Cromer workings were soon restored after World War I, the overall pattern of services was modest in relation to that pertaining in earlier years. In this context it is instructive to compare the July 1908 and July 1922 summer timetables, the results of such a comparison being as follows:

July 1908	*July 1922*
Up trains Cromer–Melton = 13	Up trains Cromer–Melton = 9
Down trains Melton–Cromer = 13	Down trains Melton–Cromer = 9

In July 1922, up trains left Cromer Beach at 7.20, 8.00, 9.35, 11.03 am, 12.10, 3.20, 6.30, 7.20 and 8.50 pm. The 9.35 am 'Leicester' stopped at Sheringham and Holt, West Runton and Weybourne being served on an 'as required' basis to take-up only. The mid-day London train (which now left Cromer at the slightly earlier time of 12.10 pm) called at all stations between Cromer and Melton Constable, but it then missed out most of the intermediate stops on the M&GN main line and reached Peterborough by 2.40 pm. Having combined with a fast express working from Newcastle it then made good time to London, with an arrival time at Kings Cross of 4.30 pm.

Down services left Melton Constable at 8.39, 9.29, 10.33 am, 12.44, 2.09, 3.51, 6.33, 6.52 and 8.04 pm, with an extra departure from Melton at 3.14 pm on Fridays and Saturdays only. Most trains called intermediately at Holt, Weybourne, Sheringham and West Runton, but the down 'Leicester' and the 3.00 pm from Kings Cross stopped at Weybourne only 'when required'; the 'Leicester' reached Cromer at 7.10 pm, while the GNR through coaches from Kings Cross arrived at 7.26 pm, giving an overall journey time of 4 hours 26 minutes from London.

The basic Cromer branch service was augmented by further main line and local trains that ran to or from Cromer and Sheringham via the Norfolk & Suffolk Joint line. There were, for instance, around half a dozen locals each way between Cromer Beach, Mundesley and North Walsham, while Great Eastern main line trains continued to reach Sheringham over the N&SJ between North Walsham, Mundesley, Newstead Lane Junction and Runton West Junction.

The 1923 Grouping

In Victorian days successive governments had resisted calls for large-scale railway amalgamations on the grounds that competition would (hopefully)

MELTON CONSTABLE and CROMER.—Midland and Great Northern Joint.

Down. Week Days.

Miles		mrn	mrn	mrn	aft	aft	aft	aft	aft	aft	aft
	Melton Constable....dep	8 50	9 45	10 40	12 20	2 50	3 58	6 6	6 58	15	
5	Holt...............	9 0	9 55	10 50	12 30	3 0	4 8	6 16	6 58	25	
8¼	Weybourne........	9 8	10 6	...	12 38	3 8	4 16	6 8	8 33	...	
11¼	Sheringham........	9 16	10 15	11 4	12 48	3 16	4 26	3 0	7 0	8 39	
13	West Runton.......	9 21	10 20	Sig 8	12 52	3 21	4 27	6 38	Sig 8	44	
15	Cromer (Beach) ¶ 326	9 26	10 25	11 11	12 57	3 26	4 32	6 40	7 8	49	

¶ 1½ miles to Great Eastern Station.

For OTHER TRAINS between Sheringham and West Runton, see page 303.

MELTON CONSTABLE and CROMER.—Midland and Great Northern Joint.

Down. Week Days only.

Miles		mrn	mrn	mrn	aft	aft	aft	aft	aft	aft
	Melton Constable.....dep	8 39	9 29	10 33	12 42	9 3	1 43	5 16	3 36	6 28 4
5	Holt...............	8 49	9 41	10 43	12 53	19 3	2 64	66	4 37	7 28 14
8¼	Weybourne........	...	3 9	51	10 51	...	4 27	3 39	...	8 22
11¼	Sheringham........	...	3 59	10 58	1 12	...	2 53	4 74	2 26	5 97 15 8 58
13	West Runton.......	...	9 3	11 2	1 21	...	2 58	47	4 37	5 14
15	Cromer (Beach) ¶ 326	arr	9 14	10 10	11 01	1 22	...	3 53	584	3 37	107 26 8 40

a Stop when required.   b Fridays and Saturdays.   d Stops when required to take up for Horwich, also for Peterboro', Bourne, and beyond.   ¶ 1¼ miles to Great Eastern Station.

For OTHER TRAINS between Sheringham and West Runton, see page 288.

MELTON CONSTABLE, SHERINGHAM and CROMER.—Midland and Great Northern Joint

Down Week Days only

Miles		mrn		N	B	E	C				
	Melton Constable..dep	52	11 40	35	27	48	45	35	1019	9 45	8 37 56	12 5

Table 48   MELTON CONSTABLE, SHERINGHAM, and CROMER (M. & G. N.)

Miles		mrn		H		
	Melton Constable. dep					

Sundays

For OTHER TRAINS between Sheringham and Cromer, page 884a.

Top Timetable for April 1910.
Second Timetable for July 1927.
Third Timetable for July 1938.
Bottom Timetable for May 1948.
All these are extracted from Bradshaw.

lead to greater efficiency. In 1853, for example, the Midland, Great Northern and London & North Western companies had approached Parliament for Powers to amalgamate, but this ambitious scheme was flatly rejected. Similarly, in 1909, the Great Northern, Great Eastern and Great Central railways had sought Powers for an amalgamation, but Parliament had again rejected the scheme. Opposition to such large scale amalgamations lessened considerably after World War I, and indeed in 1921 Parliament itself imposed a comprehensive 'grouping' scheme – this being an alternative to outright nationalisation. Thus, on 1st January, 1923, the diverse railway companies that had dominated Britain's transport system were grouped into four large undertakings, the Great Northern becoming part of the newly-created London & North Eastern Railway while the Midland was merged into the London Midland & Scottish Railway.

Unfortunately, the unplanned nature of Victorian competive capitalism had resulted in numerous anomalies that could not easily be rectified, and in this context joint lines such as the Midland & Great Northern presented especial problems. In fact, the M&GN was not 'grouped' at all because its two owning companies had passed into different organisations – the M&GN therefore remained in being as a distinct undertaking for several years after 1923, and in this respect it could be said that the Midland & Great Northern was one of the last of the pre-1923 companies (the very last main line company was the Great Northern Railway of Ireland which lasted until 1958!)

Developments in the 1930s

A visit to Cromer Beach in the 1930s would have been, in many ways, a trip into the past. The M&GN engines that worked both main line and local services retained their distinctive brown livery, while the archaic 6-wheel coaches that appeared on the branch were still lettered 'M&GN'. The only indication that grouping had taken place came with the arrival of through trains from beyond the confines of the M&GN system, for these produced LMS or LNER bogie stock – the LMS vehicles being employed on the Leicester services while their LNER counterparts worked between Cromer and Kings Cross.

Many Midland & Great Northern 6-wheelers dated from the 1880s, and all of these wooden veterans were gas lit. Most appear to have been of Great Northern origin, and photographic evidence clearly shows their characteristic 'flat-roofed' GNR profile. R.S. McNaught, who knew the M&GN at this time, described its short wheelbase coaches as 'little jolters', most of which were 'well-kept and tastefully embellished'. The oldest, he remembered, had blue lining on their varnished teak panels, while 'as befitted Puritan East Anglia, the compartments had plain white partitions without the pictures so universal over the years, and their steam heating apparatus was notorious for its angry hissing'.[7]

Another eye-witness account of the M&GN's local trains is provided by G.T. Moody, who travelled on the Cromer Beach to Mundesley route in 1923; he recalled that his three coach train was formed of three ex-GNR 6-wheelers from which the lavatory fittings had been removed. On a subsequent visit in 1924 he noticed that the Mundesley branch train was formed of two GER corridor coaches – a reminder that the Norfolk & Suffolk line was a joint M&GN/GER route![8]

In 1928 the Midland & Great Northern had around 150 short wheelbase passenger vehicles, but in the middle-1930s the parent companies transferred bogie stock to the M&GN system. The new coaches were hardly modern, but the appearance of smooth-riding bogie stock must have been welcomed by habitual travellers on the Melton to Cromer line. These bogie coaches were of various makes and vintages, though many of them were late-Victorian LNWR vehicles.

In May 1936 a *Railway Magazine* correspondent noted that 'several bogie corridor coaches of North Eastern Area type' had recently been transferred to the M&GN from the LNER. He noticed that they retained their varnished teak finish but had been lettered 'M&GN', and this suggested that the transfer was permanent. Apart from the ex-LNWR coaches referred to above, most M&GN vehicles were still 6-wheeled, and the correspondent considered that the appearance of Midland & Great Northern trains hardly tended towards uniformity – however, the stock changes were 'certainly in the interests of passenger comfort'. Other vehicles transferred in the 1930s were of Midland Railway origin, and these could easily be distinguished by their clerestory roof profiles. The ex-Midland bogie coaches were noted for their excellent suspension, but their external appearance was marred by what R.S. McNaught described as 'a coat of vile light brown paint'.

The Eastern Belle

Pullman cars did not normally appear on the Midland & Great Northern system, and it comes as something of a surprise to discover that a Pullman express regularly ran to and from Sheringham during the 1930s. The train concerned was the LNER's celebrated 'Eastern Belle' – not a scheduled service but a summer special that ran to a varied programme, taking excursionists to a range of seaside destinations throughout East Anglia. First introduced in June 1929, the 'Eastern Belle' utilised Pullman stock that the LNER had inherited in 1923, and for which there would otherwise have been no obvious use.

In 1930, the 'Eastern Belle' excursion programme featured no less than 18 different resorts including Clacton, Aldeburgh, Cromer and Hunstanton.[9] The train usually visited former Great Eastern lines, although there were occasional forays to the more distant, ex-GNR resort of Skegness. The programme changed from season to season, though some resorts were always included (Clacton was a particular favourite). Cromer was visited, on average, perhaps once a week, the station used on these occasions being the former Great Eastern terminus rather than Cromer Beach. When Sheringham was included in the excursion programme, however, the Eastern Belle reached M&GN metals via Runton West Junction, and did not call at the GER station.

The 'Eastern Belle' ran throughout the summer on every day except Saturdays (when it would have duplicated scheduled holiday trains); it usually served at least one intermediate resort in addition to the main destination, and thus, when the 'Belle' ran to Sheringham, it also called at West Runton. A typical week's running in the summer of 1934 was as follows:

Sunday	Clacton (1 hour 30 minutes)
Monday	Wroxham, North Walsham & Cromer (2 hours 58 minutes)
Tuesday	Thorpeness & Aldeburgh (1 hour 30 minutes)
Wednesday	Clacton (1 hour 30 minutes)
Thursday	Wroxham, West Runton & Sheringham (3 hours 30 minutes)
Friday	Skegness (3 hours 25 minutes)

The third class return fare from London to Sheringham was 7s. 6d. inclusive of the Pullman supplement, while for 37s. 6d. one could buy a weekly season for use throughout the week. The first class return fare to Sheringham was 12s. 6d., while a full *table d'hôte* Pullman Lunch was available at 2s. 6d. for third class and 3s. for first class travellers.

The train was usually composed of seven or eight chocolate and cream Pullman vehicles, one of which would be first class; in the mid-1930s these were often *Albion, Fortuna* or *Calais*. These Pullman excursions were always well patronised, and older people recall the 'Eastern Belle' concept as a highlight of pre-war summer operation. The 'Eastern Belle' was, however, merely one of the many excursions that ran over the M & GN Cromer branch during the 1920s and 1930s.

In general, excursion traffic on the Cromer Beach line originated, not in London, but in the Midlands. London traffic generally ran to and from the GER station, and although the opening of the Norfolk & Suffolk Joint line had enabled through trains from London to reach Sheringham, the Midland & Great Northern system remained pre-eminent as a holiday link between central England and the Norfolk coast. Moreover, rising standards of living (among those with jobs) meant that increasing numbers of working class families were able to spend one or two weeks beside the sea each year, and for this reason coastal lines such as the M & GN became exceptionally busy during the summer months.

Summer Saturdays presented special problems in terms of holiday traffic, the basic operational problem being compounded by the long stretches of single line on the Midland & Great Northern system. Some idea of the volume of holiday traffic at this time will be apparent when one considers that on 6th August, 1932 no less than 24 packed holiday trains passed through Melton Constable from Cromer or Great Yarmouth: 17 of these were through workings to the LMS system, while the remaining 7 were bound for destinations on the London & North Eastern Railway.[10]

Freight Traffic

Like all seaside lines, the Melton Constable to Cromer branch carried a heavy summer passenger traffic, but it also served the needs of local communities such as Weybourne, Holt, Sheringham, and a host of neighbouring villages and hamlets. Country stations were designed as railheads for the surrounding area, and in the days when all journeys were by train and most commodities were moved by rail, the role of stations such as Holt or

Weybourne cannot be over-estimated. Holt, for instance, served the residents of Baconsthorpe, Hempstead, Hunworth, Little Thornage, Letheringsett, Wiveton, Glandford, Salthouse and Kelling – horse-drawn transport being used to convey goods and passengers to and from the railhead. Gentry could use their own vehicles to reach the nearest station, while humbler folk might ride on a convenient carrier's cart (most country carriers adhered to clearly-defined routes and worked to regular timetables). Farmers used their lumbering Norfolk wagons to convey hay or other produce to the station, though two-wheeled carts would typically be used to transport milk churns to and from the railway.

The freight traffic carried reflected the economy of the immediate locality, corn or root crops being valuable sources of freight, while milk production became increasingly important during the 20th century. East Anglia was not a specialised dairy farming region, but the opening of railways such as the M & GN enabled local farmers to cater for the vast London market, and most stations handled large quantities of milk churns.

The actual volume of milk traffic was greater than might be expected, and it is possible to obtain some idea of the importance of this form of traffic with the aid of a bundle of milk waybills, fortuitously discovered in the cellar at Melton Constable station prior to its demolition. These waybills all relate to the months of January and February 1926 and they show a variety of useful information – it is, in particular, possible to identify the consignors, the consignee(s) and the number of gallons sent in each can. Some of this data has been incorporated in the following table, which gives details of milk traffic from Melton Constable for the period 16th January, 1926 to 15th February, 1926 inclusive.

Milk consignment note for 27th January, 1926.

Table 2

MILK TRAFFIC FROM MELTON CONSTABLE JANUARY–FEBRUARY 1926

Date	Gallons	Name of Consignee	Destination
16th Jan.	10	The Dairy Supply Co.	Finsbury Park
17th Jan.	46	Messrs Welford	Finsbury Park
18th Jan.	75	United Dairies	Finsbury Park
	10	The Dairy Supply Co.	Finsbury Park
22nd Jan.	68	The Dairy Supply Co.	Stratford
23rd Jan.	6	United Dairies	Finsbury Park
25th Jan.	12	The Dairy Supply Co.	Finsbury Park
26th Jan.	6	United Dairies	Finsbury Park
	102	London CWS Ltd	Finsbury Park
			Stratford
27th Jan.	24	Messrs Welford	Finsbury Park
29th Jan.	31	{Messrs Welford	Finsbury Park
	12	{The Dairy Supply Co.	Finsbury Park
30th Jan.	34	{London CWS Ltd	Stamford Hill
	62	{United Dairies	Finsbury Park
1st Feb.	13	{The Dairy Supply Co.	Finsbury Park
	33	{Messrs Welford	Finsbury Park
2nd Feb.	34	London CWS Ltd	Stamford Hill
4th Feb.	14	The Dairy Supply Co.	Finsbury Park
8th Feb.	34	Messrs Welford	Finsbury Park
9th Feb.	11	The Dairy Supply Co.	Finsbury Park
10th Feb.	6	United Dairies	Finsbury Park
15th Feb.	64	United Dairies	Finsbury Park

It will be seen that all of the milk sent from Melton Constable was destined for consumption in London, and – significantly – much of it was sent to Finsbury Park on the Great Northern line. A few consignments were destined for Stratford or Stamford Hill (both on the GER system), but most of the milk traffic from Melton Constable in this sample period was routed via Peterborough and the Great Northern main line – which was, after all, the natural outlet for M&GN traffic to the metropolis.

Study of the above table will show that the average quantity of milk sent each day from Melton Constable was 44½ gallons, and by applying this figure to the whole branch one might reasonably assume that stations on the Cromer line were sending upwards of 200 gallons of milk a day. This figure is not, particularly high, though it should be remembered that the yield in January would be low compared with the amount of milk produced during the summer months. Research carried out in relation to the Fairford line[11] suggests that a Great Western station such as Witney sent around 225 gallons of milk each day to London, but M&GN stations are unlikely to have handled as much as this, even during the productive months of Spring. Nevertheless, Norfolk is not generally associated with dairy farming, and in this sense the figure of 44 gallons a day may come as a surprise to those who think that the rasp and clatter of 17 gallon churns was heard only on the Great Western Railway!

If milk traffic was higher than expected it must be admitted that the amount of fish carried on the M & GN Cromer branch was (apparently) rather low. In general the Midland & Great Northern conveyed large quantities of fresh fish from Lowestoft and Great Yarmouth, but there was less opportunity for the Joint Committee to develop comparable traffic from Cromer or Sheringham. The absence of proper harbour facilities at these two places meant that fishing was carried out on a small scale, and in any case, local fishermen specialised in crab or lobster fishing – most of their catches being sold locally to holidaymakers. There was, nevertheless, at least some scope for the conveyance of 'Cromer crabs' by rail, while in the reverse direction fish offal was sent from Lowestoft for use as bait by Cromer fishermen. Edgar J. March has recorded that the offal was 'retailed in small hampers to the Cromer fishermen at an average price of 5s. each, including carriage. One hamper baited 40 pots, which had to be fresh baited every day'.[12]

Fish waybills in the author's collection show that boxes of fish weighing up to 74 lb. were regularly sent from Lowestoft to Melton Constable, and there were occasional consignments of fish from Hull. It is assumed that these consignments were of cod, herring or other types of white fish that may not always have been obtainable locally, but whatever types of fish were involved it comes as something of a surprise to discover fish being sent from Hull to north Norfolk!

If the fish traffic from Cromer and Sheringham was modest in relation to that emanating from Yarmouth, Lowestoft or other large-scale fishing ports, one must not forget that the maintenance of a working fishing fleet, however small, required a ready supply of timber, ironwork, fastenings, ropes, blocks and paint, and many of these items would have been sent out to Cromer or Sheringham by rail. Local boat builders such as John Johnson or Robert Emery (both of Sheringham) carried out a flourishing trade during the days of sail, and the existence of such firms must have ensured a steady flow of small freight traffic to Cromer and Sheringham stations.

Although the combined quantities of milk, fish and general merchandise carried over the Melton to Cromer branch would have been significant, the profits accruing from such traffic were small; milk churns, parcels and small freight consignments needed constant handling, and the distances covered were often minimal. Wagon load traffic, in contrast, was a more profitable type of business, coal being the one guaranteed source of bulk freight traffic on the Cromer line. At a time when coal was widely used for domestic heating, most small country stations had coal wharves used by local coal merchants, and there were, in addition, one or two industrial users. Sheringham gas works, for instance, was coal-fired, while Cromer gas works had its own railway siding; also rail-connected was the Cromer Electricity Works, and this, too, brought welcome wagon load coal traffic to an otherwise passenger-orientated branch.

Cromer and the other branch stations were adequately equipped to deal with coal, cattle and most other forms of freight traffic, and apart from West Runton (which was a passenger-only station) all of the stations had goods yards containing loading docks, cattle pens and coal wharves. Fixed hand cranes were available at Cromer and Melton Constable, but not at the smaller stations.

The types of traffic that could be handled at each station are shown in the following table, which was compiled with the aid of successive editions of the *Railway Clearing House Handbook of Stations*. The table is probably self-explanatory, but it may be worth pointing out that 'L' indicates the presence of a cattle dock at which livestock could be handled, while 'F', 'H' and 'C' show that the stations referred to were equipped with raised loading docks in which furniture, vans, horse boxes or machinery wagons could be accommodated. For convenience, all of the private sidings are shown, though not all of these were in use at the same time.

Table 3

STATION ACCOMMODATION AND PRIVATE SIDINGS c.1900–30

Stations	m. ch.	Facilities	Crane	Private Sidings
Melton Constable	00 00	G P F L H C	1 ton	Melton Gas Works
Holt	05 11	G P F L H C	—	Norfolk County Council
				Kelling Ballast Pit
Weybourne	08 55	G P F L H C	—	—
Sheringham	11 30	G P F L H C	—	—
West Runton	13 07	P	—	—
Cromer Beach	15 16	G P F L H C	1 ton	Cromer Gas Works
				Cromer Electricity Works
				Cromer Urban District C

Key G = Goods & Minerals; P = Passengers & Parcels; F = Loading Dock for furniture, machinery etc; L = Cattle & Livestock; H = Horses & Prize Cattle; C = Cars & Carriages by Passenger Train.

Although it is possible to gain some understanding of the types of goods traffic over rural lines such as the Melton to Cromer branch, it is often difficult to know what kinds of wagons would have been used at country stations on a day-to-day basis. Photographs provide a clue – though one can never know if a shot of a particular goods yard at a given time is presenting a typical picture. On the other hand, the types of traffic carried would, to some extent, have dictated what rolling stock was used, and for this reason it is safe to assume that ordinary open wagons would have predominated in the make-up of most M&GN goods trains. Such vehicles would have carried coal or other bulk minerals, together with hay (under sheets), timber and heavy items such as sectionalised drain pipes. Many wagons were M&GN vehicles carrying the Midland & Great Northern's own livery, but LMS and LNER vehicles were also used on a regular basis.

General merchandise traffic was conveyed in covered vans, while machinery and other heavy equipment was carried on simple flat wagons. One speciality on the Cromer line was, of course, fish traffic, and this perishable commodity was transported in special fish vans that were, in many cases, attached to convenient passenger trains. This practice persisted for many years, although, by the 1930s, the insidious growth of road transport had led to a decrease in the amount of fish despatched from Cromer or Sheringham by rail.

The LNER Takeover

Fish traffic was not the only sphere of M&GN operations to be affected by road competition during the 1930s, and like all rural railways, the Midland & Great Northern soon felt the effects of this rival form of transport. At the same time, an underlying trade depression had contributed to a regime of retrenchment on all British railways, and against this background of economic difficulty it became clear that the jointly-operated M&GN was an anachronism. Consequently, on 1st October, 1936, the LMS and LNER companies modified the long-standing arrangements under which the 183½ mile M&GN system was operated, and responsibility for the line was taken over by the LNER.

The LNER lost no time in implementing a series of economies throughout the Midland & Great Northern system, one of the first changes being the closure of Melton Constable works in December 1936. The M&GN locomotive fleet passed into LNER ownership, and the prefix '0' was added to the existing M&GN numbers. Sadly, many former Midland & Great Northern engines were scrapped within the first months of LNER ownership, and the 'Locomotive Notes' pages of the *Railway Magazine* reveal a sorry catalogue of withdrawals; in May 1937, for instance, the magazine reported the demise of two Beyer, Peacock class 'A' 4−4−0s, one class 'D' 0−6−0 and no less than eight class 'C' 4−4−0s.

In general, the LNER takeover resulted in the rapid elimination of the former Midland & Great Northern locomotive fleet, but whereas GER or GNR types were provided for work on the M&GN main line, the branch lines remained – at least for a few years – bastions of M&GN influence. On a typical day's running in January 1937, for example, the 12.35 pm service from Melton Constable to Cromer Beach was worked by Marriott 4−4−2T No. 09, while the 3.00 pm up working was hauled by Sharp, Stewart class 'C' 4−4−0 No. 02 (a veteran locomotive dating back to 1894!) Another Sharp, Stewart 4−4−0 used on the Cromer branch at this time was No. 012 which, in July 1938, was noted entering Cromer Beach at the head of a four coach local working.

The train service provided under LNER auspices was generally similar to that offered to the travelling public prior to October 1936. There were still around 12−13 passenger trains in each direction between Melton Constable and Cromer Beach. In July 1938 up trains left Cromer Beach at 8.00, 8.55, 9.40, 11.40 am and 12.10, 2.05, 3.00, 5.43, 6.35, 7.30 and 9.20 pm, with additional departures on Fridays and Mondays. In the reverse direction, up trains left Melton at 7.11, 8.40, 9.35, 10.27 am, and 12.45, 2.10, 4.09, 4.58, 6.37, 6.56 and 6.10 pm – the first train of the day being a through service to Liverpool Street via Cromer GER station. As in the up direction, extra trains ran on Fridays and Mondays to cater for weekend travellers.

Through trains still ran to and from Kings Cross and Leicester, but the appearance of a service from Melton to Liverpool Street was the most significant feature of the 1938 timetable. This train (first introduced in 1937) ran throughout the year, giving through travellers to London an alternative to the long-established 12.10 pm to Kings Cross.

Operation in World War Two

The outbreak of World War II on 3rd September, 1939 led to an immediate cut in train services. Through workings were severely curtailed, the 7.11 am from Melton to Liverpool Street and the 12.10 pm from Cromer to Kings Cross being among the first casualties of the 1939–45 conflict. Another victim was the popular 9.40 am 'Leicester', which did not run during the 1939–45 war (although it had been maintained throughout World War I). Branch train services between Cromer Beach and Mundesley were initially reduced to just three workings each way, but in December 1939 the service was increased to four up and four down workings.

Despite the cut in train services, the Melton to Cromer route was called upon to carry large numbers of servicemen to and from military establishments in the Cromer area. There were, for example, large army camps at Weybourne and at Stiffkey (near Holt), and both of these installations brought extra traffic to the railway. The Royal Air Force also became well-established in Norfolk during the dark days of World War II, one of the many RAF stations in this coastal area being at Langham, to the north-west of Holt. Langham aerodrome was (by 1944) part of Coastal Command, and its aircraft allocation consisted of two squadrons of Beaufighters manned by Australian and New Zealand airmen.

Although the first months of war had been so uneventful that people had spoken dismissively of a 'Phoney War', the sudden and unexpected capitulation of France in May–June 1940 had thrust the Cromer area into the exposed front line of a major European conflict. The British Army had itself been defeated in France, and, in the summer and autumn of 1940, the country was defended by the RAF and the Navy – helped by an eccentric organisation known as the 'Local Defence Volunteers' (soon renamed the Home Guard). A major problem, at this critical time, was Britain's acute shortage of military vehicles – much vital equipment having been destroyed in France. One answer to this problem was the creation of a fleet of armoured trains for use in threatened coastal areas, and at least one of these units was active in the Cromer area.

The train consisted of specially-armoured 'F4' 2–4–2T No. 7189, flanked by two personnel carriers and two gun wagons. The whole ensemble was encased in quarter inch steel plate, and its offensive armament included rifles, machine guns and naval-type six pounders than could be trained fore and aft. The train carried a crew of 26, including locomen, gunners, one officer, one NCO and a wireless operator.

There were, in all, a total of 12 such trains, (together with several spares) and each unit was distinguished by an alphabetic code-letter; the train normally used on the lines to Cromer and Melton Constable was 'Train G', though other units may also have appeared at various times during the invasion scare of 1940–41. (Sadly, the trains were rarely photographed; this was, at least in part, for security reasons, but many of their patrols were nocturnal, and this was hardly conducive to successful photography!)

Most serious historians now agree that Hitler never seriously intended to invade the British Isles, but this reassuring fact was by no means clear in 1940, and when, on 4th September, an invasion alert was accidently sent out the 'defenders' of Cromer (many of them naval personnel) were ordered to man their trenches above the beach!

Happily, the 4th September alert was a false alarm, and although Cromer was attacked by the Luftwaffe during the war, the first, critical stage of the 1939–45 conflict was brought to an end when the Germans turned their full attention to Russia. Thereafter, as the British war effort got into its stride, preparations were made for the eventual liberation of Europe. Local rail services were gradually improved during this period, and there were, by May 1943, eight up and eight down workings between Melton and Cromer. This meagre service could hardly be compared to the pre-war summer timetables, but there were, nevertheless, one or two interesting features of wartime passenger operation. Some trains ran into the former Great Eastern station in order to give useful connections to Norwich or London, while Sheringham gained special significance as an interchange point between the M&GN and GER systems.

Of even greater significance was the way in which through services to Liverpool Street (rather than Kings Cross) were re-introduced. In May 1943, for instance, the 6.30 am from Melton Constable proceeded to Norwich and thence to Liverpool Street after calling at the former GER station in Cromer; in the reverse direction, the last train of the day worked through from London, with an arrival time at Melton of 10.23 pm. This service was especially appreciated by servicemen who could, by travelling out on the morning train and returning in the evening, spend a day in London.

Norwich was, of course, a popular place for servicemen to visit for an evening's entertainment, and in this context it is interesting to find that a special Saturday evening late night train was provided between Norwich Thorpe, North Walsham, Mundesley and thence to Cromer Beach. The former M&GN route via Melton Constable, Hindolveston and Norwich City was of less use because the connections at Melton Constable were virtually non-existent; the last down service from Melton to Cromer, for example, left at 9.45 pm, nearly two hours after the arrival of the 7.12 pm from Norwich City. There was, it is true, a late night Saturday train from Norwich City to Melton Constable at 11.15 pm, but this arrived in Melton at 11.55 pm, long after the Cromer service had departed.

On the motive power front the war years were a period of major change. As we have seen, the Cromer branch had retained at least some of its former Midland & Great Northern flavour during the later 1930s, but sadly, most of the surviving M&GN locomotives were withdrawn during the 1939–45 war. Class 'C' 4–4–0 No. 012, for example, was broken-up in 1942 while sister engines Nos. 02 and 042 were scrapped in the following year. By the end of the war, very few Midland & Great Northern engines remained, and the lines to Cromer and Mundesley were worked by an assortment of 'foreign' types from the GER or GNR. These included ex-Great Eastern 'F3' or 'F4' 2–4–2Ts, 'J15' 0–6–0s and Ivatt 4–4–0s from the former Great Northern system.

The practice of running M&GN trains in and out of the Great Eastern station at Cromer may have given wartime travellers a useful range of connections, but there were operational problems in that these workings had to stop at Cromer Junction and then reverse along the GER line prior to resuming their journeys. This operation was a source of alarm for nervous travellers – especially when the trains ran backwards at considerable speed! The Appendix to the May 1942 Working Timetable reveals that passenger workings of up to ten bogie coaches could be propelled from Cromer Junction into the station if piloted by a 'competent man'.

Cromer's old fashioned High Street, with the Parish Church of Saints Peter & Paul in the background as seen from an old postcard.　　*Oakwood Collection*

LNER 4–4–0 No. 043 entering Melton Constable from Cromer on 13th March, 1939. *H.C. Casserley*

An interesting view of Ivatt class 'J3' 0–6–0 No. 82 (*left*) and Johnson class 'D' 0–6–0 No. 68 at Melton Constable in 1937 (outside East signal box). The Ivatt class locomotives were used mainly on the western section of the M&GN but they were also seen from time to time at Melton. *H.C. Casserley*

The Melton down home signals (Kings Lynn line) were carried on an impressive concrete gantry; in its heyday this assembly sported 5 arms.   *H.N. James*

Another concrete signal at the west end of Melton Constable station.

E.R. Morton

An M & GNR notice at Melton Constable.

H.N. Turner

Typical M&GNR somersault signals at Sheringham. H.N. James

Melton home signal (Norwich line).
H.N. James

Concrete-posted somersault signals near Briningham Crossing. H.N. James

The west end of Melton Constable station, showing the Cromer line diverging to the right, and the M & GNR main line to the left. *H.C. Casserley*

Sharp, Stewart class 'C' 4–4–0 No. 43 (as LNER No. 043) glides round the sharp curves at the west end of Melton Constable station on 13th March, 1939. The train includes former GER Van No. 84966 (built 1906), an M & GNR van, plus an assortment of ex-LNWR passenger stock. *H.C. Casserley*

A general view of Melton Constable station looking towards Norwich. Lord Hastings's private waiting room is visible to the right and the coaling stage can be seen in the middle distance; the date is c.1957.   *Mowat Collection*

The miniature waiting room provided at Melton for the exclusive use of Lord Hastings was, in effect, a private station on its own short length of platform.

E.R. Morton

A general view of Melton Constable station, looking east towards Yarmouth.
Lens of Sutton

Although taken after closure, this c.1967 view of the overbridge at the western end of Melton Constable station provides a useful view of the fully enclosed stairway that gave access to the island platform.
Author

nother post-closure ew of Melton Constable ation, showing the ysterious 'Central orfolk Railway' iron- ork and the trap door hich marked the posi- on of the station llars. Lord Hastings's aiting room is in the ft distance. *Author*

Melton Constable station looking west during the Edwardian era. The waiting room/toilet block visible to the right was subsequently rebuilt with an outer casing of concrete blocks.

Oakwood Collection

Chapter Five
The Stations and Route

The preceding chapters have examined the early history and subsequent development of the Midland & Great Northern branch to Cromer, but little has been said in relation to the physical appearance of the line. The following section will therefore take readers on an imaginary 'guided tour' of the route from Melton Constable to Cromer Beach. Generally speaking, the topographical details that follow will be correct for the post-1937 periods, although there may be one or two references to earlier or later periods.

Melton Constable Station and Works

Situated at the hub of four converging lines, Melton Constable was, in truth, the operational centre of the Midland & Great Northern system – its significance being underlined by the presence of the company's locomotive and carriage works and a busy engine shed.

In terms of passenger traffic, Melton Constable was an important junction. Many M&GN trains conveyed through portions for Lowestoft, Yarmouth or Cromer, and it was normal for these workings to be divided at Melton Constable – the usual practice being for Cromer portions to be worked onto the branch after the main Norwich or Yarmouth sections had departed. Unusually, there were no branch bays, and all trains arrived or departed from a long island platform with through tracks on either side. There was ample room for trains to be coupled-up or divided, the two faces of the island platform each being around 800 ft long.

Access to and from the island platform was by means of a covered stairway that descended from an adjacent road overbridge. The stairs connected with a long, single-storey station building containing the usual booking office and a well-stocked refreshment room; the main station building was covered by a pitched roof which continued, at its eastern end, as an open *loggia* supported on cylindrical iron columns. An interesting feature of this structure was the use of metal spandrels bearing the initials 'CNR' (an intriguing legacy of the abortive Central Norfolk Railway scheme).

The station building was built in attractive yellow brickwork, and its exterior woodwork was adorned (in LNER days) in a two-tone green and cream colour scheme. Minor architectural details included the usual ornate Victorian barge boards and fretwork decoration – although the overall effect was (at least by 19th century standards) restrained.

Other buildings on the main island platform provided public waiting room and toilet facilities, the former being situated in a single-storey block at the eastern end of the main building. Interestingly, some of the space beneath the island platform was adapted for use as a cellar, trap doors in the platform surface being used to give access to this underground storage area. To the south of the passenger station, a small brick building standing on its own section of platform provided private waiting room facilities for Lord Hastings and his family.

Melton works was situated to the south of the railway, and observant travellers were able to obtain a good view of this small, but efficient en-

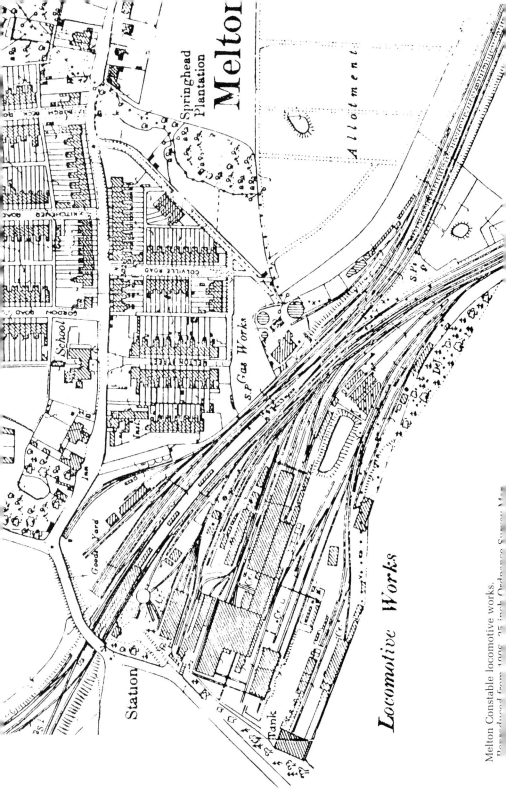

Melton Constable locomotive works.

Reproduced from 1906 25 inch Ordnance Survey Map

gineering establishment as they waited on the adjacent passenger platform. Opened in 1883, the works had been added to and extended over the years, and by the 1920s it provided a wide range of facilities including a locomotive shop, a carriage and wagon shop, a paint shop and a machine shop.

Access to the locomotive works was by means of a headshunt connection beside the Melton to Norwich line, a reverse shunt being necessary in order that locomotives or rolling stock could enter or leave the works yard. There were around a dozen sidings within the yard, and many of these entered the works buildings so that repairs could be accomplished under cover (in earlier days, however, some work had taken place in the open air). The various works buildings were constructed of brick, the main workshops being sited end-to-end at the very centre of the complex; this central range of buildings was almost a quarter of a mile long. Other buildings were situated to the north and south of the central range, and these too were rail-connected.

The largest workshops were the locomotive shops, and the carriage and wagon shop, their overall dimensions being 120 ft × 125 ft and 150 ft × 80 ft respectively. In common with other Victorian-style engineering factories, the lathes, drills and other machine tools were powered by a system of overhead shafts, belt drives being employed to transfer power to the individual machines. The erecting shop was equipped with an overhead gantry crane, by means of which heavy components could easily be lifted during locomotive repair or building work.

In theory, Melton was a locomotive repair establishment, though as we have seen the three locally-designed 4–4–2 tanks were virtually new construction. In reality, the William Marriott and his workforce carried out several major rebuilding operations at Melton, starting in the 1890s when some of the Cornwall Minerals 0–6–0s were turned into useful 2–4–0 tank engines. The first of these major conversions took place in 1890 when No. 18 was re-wheeled and adapted in various other ways; Nos. 3, 13 and 14 were similarly altered in 1891–92. Later, components from the former CMR engines were utilised in a new class of nine 0–6–0Ts, all of which were built at Melton between 1897 and 1905.

Other major work undertaken at Melton Constable included the reboilering of the M&GN's 4–4–0 and 0–6–0 engines so that, like their counterparts on the Midland Railway, these locomotives were progressively rebuilt and enlarged. In general, the rebuilt engines resembled those on the Midland proper – though it should be remembered that these major reconstructions were accomplished, not in the vastness of Derby locomotive works but in a small workshop in the middle of rural Norfolk!

For locomotive enthusiasts, the works was of particular interest in that the entire Midland & Great Northern locomotive fleet visited the establishment at one time or another, and until 1936 one could usually be sure of seeing a representative selection of the M&GN's diverse collection of motive power in or around the works yard.

Also of interest was the running shed, which occupied a wedge of land between the works and the passenger station. The shed was a rectangular structure measuring approximately 120 ft × 40 ft and containing three dead-

Melton Constable station looking west towards Kings Lynn during the British
Railways era. The waiting room block (*centre*) has now been clad in concrete but
otherwise the scene had changed little since the M & GNR period *Douglas Thompson*

A general view of Melton Constable station, looking west towards Kings Lynn with
the locomotive works on the left. *Lens of Sutton*

end roads. It was built of brick, the side walls being formed of a series of low-crowned arches filled with small-paned windows, while the front gable was of timber construction. Ten prominent smoke vents lined the low-pitched roof, and there was a lean-to extension at the rear.

The shed provided covered accommodation for up to 12 engines, but there were, in addition, two parallel engine storage roads on each side of the building and locomotives could often be seen (or photographed) on these 'outside' roads. Another siding branched out to serve the adjacent turntable, and (in later years at least) there was a headshunt connection to the works. The turntable was also accessible from the station and it was possible, by means of a series of reverse shunts, for engines to back onto the table and then proceed to the shed or works.

Melton Constable goods yard was situated on the north side of the passenger station, entry from the running lines being by means of a series of parallel loops and headshunts. The yard contained several lengthy sidings; those on the southern side (i.e. nearest the station) were used mainly for storage or re-marshalling work, while two long sidings in the centre of the yard were available for loading or unloading purposes. Other sidings extended along the northern edge of the goods yard area, and these too were used for the loading or unloading of coal or other commodities. There were, in all, seven long sidings (including the 'marshalling' roads) together with a number of short dead end spurs. The goods yard contained the usual loading docks and coal wharves, and a 1 ton crane was available for use when timber or other large consignments were transferred between road and rail vehicles.

The railway workers lived in typical Victorian terraced houses on the north side of the station complex. Melton Constable was an archetypal railway village, and although it had been in existence long before the coming of the Lynn & Fakenham Railway, the modern village was not built until the 1880s and 1890s. The first houses were ready for occupation by 1882, and thereafter the railway village spread rapidly. Streets such as 'Gordon Road', and 'Kitchener Road' testified to the late-Victorian origins of the settlement, while the Hastings Arms Hotel commemorated the part played by Lord Hastings who, as resident landowner, willingly co-operated with the Lynn & Fakenham company and its successors. By 1901 the population of Melton Constable had reached 934, whereas in 1881 (i.e. before the railway) the original village had been home to just 118 people.

Amenities in Melton Constable village included shops, a mechanics' institute and a school, the whole settlement being lit by gas supplied from the M&GN gas works at the bottom of Melton Street. Needless to say, this gas plant was supplied by rail, coal for the retort house being brought in by means of a siding connection from the adjacent goods yard headshunt.

The station and junctions were controlled from just two signal boxes which were strategically-sited at each end of the station and known as Melton East and Melton West boxes. The signals were of typical Midland & Great Northern design with centre-pivotted 'somersault' arms mounted on square posts that were, in some cases, moulded from concrete. Indeed, the use of concrete as a general-purpose building material was a Midland & Great Northern speciality, and part of Melton works was fitted-out as a

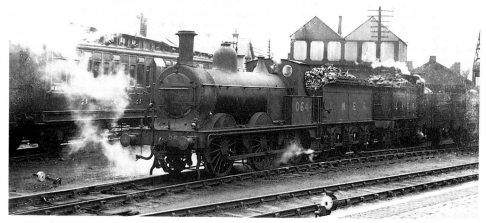

Johnson class 'D' 0−6−0 goods engine No. 64 (as LNER No. 064) simmering gently in the locomotive yard at Melton Constable on 14th March, 1939.   *H.C. Casserley*

A concrete milepost at Melton Constable works.   *E.R. Morton*

(18—V19)

MIDLAND & GREAT NORTHERN RAILWAYS JOINT COMMITTEE.

TO

MELTON CONSTABLE

'concrete shop' for the large scale production of concrete mouldings, posts
and building blocks. In this context it is interesting to note that a large gantry
carrying the Melton down home signals (Kings Lynn line) was said to be 'the
largest concrete signal in the world'; this unusual assembly incorporated
five signal arms, one of which was a Midland-style hammer-headed calling-
on arm that allowed incoming trains to enter the station during shunting
operations.

Further evidence of the use of concrete was provided by the road overbridge at the western end of the station; at first glance this appeared to be a
normal stone or grey brick structure, but closer examination revealed that
the bridge was fabricated with the aid of rectangular blocks of concrete.
Produced in the nearby works, these blocks were shaped to look like
stonework; they were laid in regular courses, larger castings being used as
lintels and copings. The bridge had two full spans, and the hollow central
pier contained a small store for platform trolleys, platelayers' tools or other
pieces of equipment.

The closure of Melton works, which took place in December 1936,
obviously resulted in a diminuation in the level of activity at Melton Constable. The locomotive sheds remained in being, however, and small scale
repair work was still carried out locally. Moreover, Melton remained an
important junction, and its extensive stabling facilities were still needed in
connection (for example) with the through London to Sheringham services –
many of which continued to Melton Constable as empty stock workings after
passengers had disembarked at Cromer or Sheringham.

Leaving Melton Constable, Cromer-bound trains passed beneath the concrete overbridge at the western end of the station and immediately diverged
to the right onto the Cromer line. Entering a cutting, the double track line
commenced a great curve towards the north, and with Melton West box
visible to the left, trains set off on their journey to the sea. Having gained a
northerly heading, the line passed over a brief stretch of embankment,
beyond which the double line converged with a minor road as it neared the
village of Briningham.

Holt

Passing over a gated level crossing, the railway skirted the village before
reaching Briningham signal box. Situated just 1 mile 4 chains from Melton
Constable, this isolated cabin controlled an adjacent level crossing, and it
also marked the end of the double line – the sections beyond being predominantly single track with crossing loops at the stations.

With Briningham receding into the distance the route curved north-
eastwards, and, with the B1110 road running parallel to the right, trains
approached a further stretch of embankment. A single span bridge carried
the line across the B1110, and the route then crossed the minor road from
Thornage to Stody on a somewhat similar bridge. Beyond this, the railway
passed through more cuttings prior to emerging on another embankment.
Crossing a minor road and a small stream, the railway meandered northwards once more as it followed the Glaven Valley on its circuitous course
towards the North Sea.

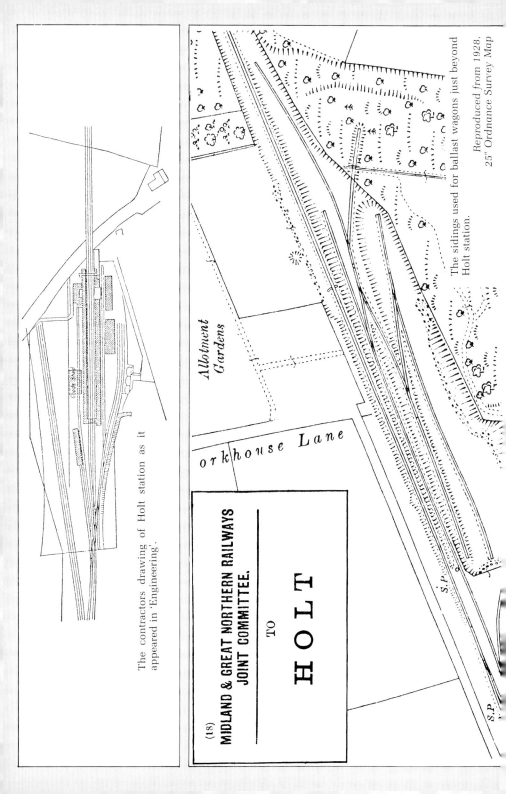

The contractors drawing of Holt station as it appeared in 'Engineering'.

(18)
MIDLAND & GREAT NORTHERN RAILWAYS
JOINT COMMITTEE.

TO

HOLT

Reproduced from 1928,
25" Ordnance Survey Map

The sidings used for ballast wagons just beyond Holt station.

Allotment
Gardens

orkhouse Lane

Goods Shed

S.P.

S.P.

Holt station, looking east towards Cromer; the station buildings here were substantially rebuilt after a fire.   *Douglas Thompson*

A closer view of the signal cabin and level crossing at Holt on 21st February, 1959. The ballast sidings can be seen in the middle distance on the right of the running lines (*see map opposite*).   *Lens of Sutton*

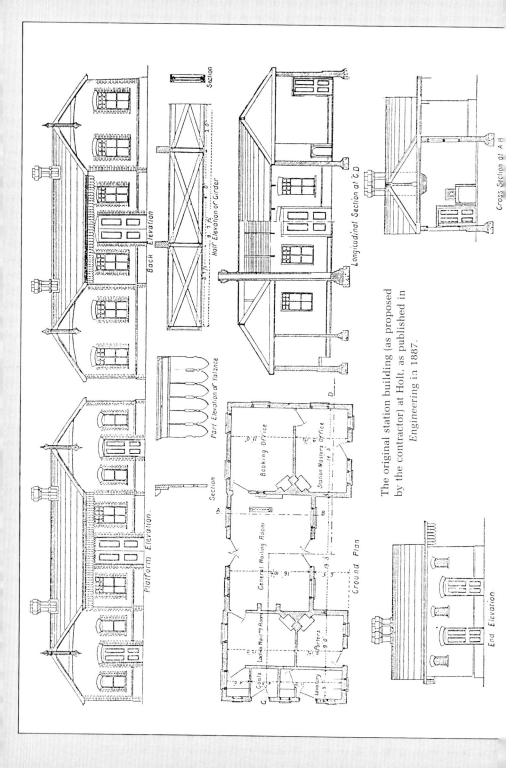

The original station building (as proposed by the contractor) at Holt, as published in Engineering in 1887.

Running through pleasant rural countryside, trains passed beneath the B1110 for a second time, and with embankments following cuttings in quick succession, the line turned north-eastwards as it neared Holt. Climbing steadily at 1 in 90 the route passed over 'Common Hill', and having emerged from a series of cuttings trains came to a stand in the lengthy crossing loop at Holt.

Situated some 5 miles 11 chains from Melton Constable, Holt was a two-platform station with substantial brick buildings on the down platform and a small waiting shelter on the up side. There were several dead-end sidings here, and the B1149 road crossed the line on the level at the eastern end of the platforms.

Holt was the terminus of the line from October 1884 until June 1887, but little remained of the original 1884 station; its sleeper platform and simple wooden buildings were soon replaced by more durable structures which (like most features of the M&GN system) had probably been designed by William Marriott. The brick-built station building was of recognizable Midland & Great Northern design, with a central block and two projecting cross wings – the central portion being set back from the gabled cross wings to form a small *loggia* for waiting passengers.* (Amusingly, the original wooden station building later found a new lease of life as a 'reading room' at Melton Constable!)

The waiting shelter on the up platform was another characteristic Midland & Great Northern design featuring a generously-proportioned platform canopy with typical Victorian-style saw tooth decoration. In M&GN days, external woodwork was painted in a brown-and-buff colour scheme – the canopies being picked-out in contrasting light and dark shades.

Holt's crossing loop and siding connections were, in earlier days, controlled from an abnormally-tall signal cabin. This towering structure was situated on the up platform, and its height must have given signalmen a clear view over the adjacent waiting shelter. In later years, a new box was erected at the eastern end of the up platform, in which position it was conveniently-sited in relation to the B1149 level crossing; this later box was of Great Northern design, with small-paned windows and ornate scalloped barge boards.

Other features at Holt included a small, concrete-faced lock-up on the down platform, together with the usual collection of huts and permanent way cabins. The platforms were fenced with typical M&GN-pattern slatted fencing and in summertime the station gardens were the setting for some attractive floral displays.

The first station master here was probably George Ridley, but Mr Ridley had left Holt by 1896, and in his place the station was supervised by William Whistler, who remained for many years and was still in office around 1912–14. A later station master, around 1920–25, was John Say, while in 1926 the station master was W.J. Munson.

One reason why M&GN station masters such as William Whistler worked for so long at one station was that, on a small system such as the Midland & Great Northern, there were few opportunities for further promotion; on the

---

*The *loggia* was later bricked-in, while even greater changes ensued when the entire building was rebuilt after a major fire.

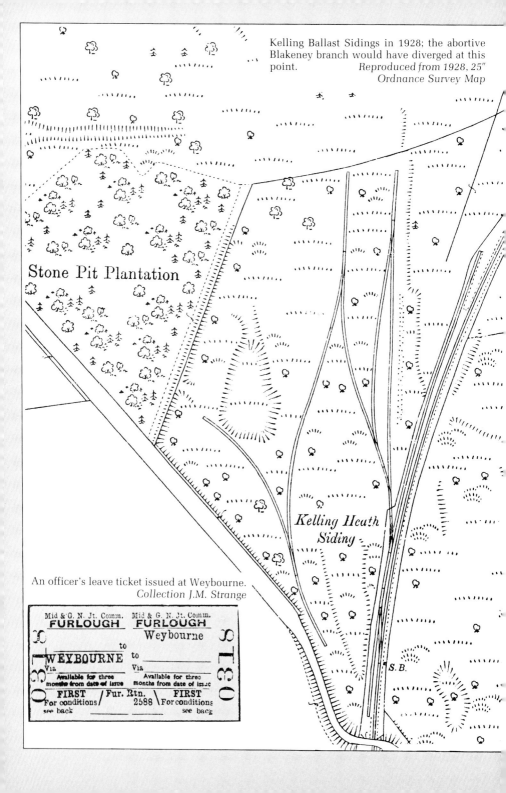

Kelling Ballast Sidings in 1928; the abortive Blakeney branch would have diverged at this point. *Reproduced from 1928, 25" Ordnance Survey Map*

Stone Pit Plantation

Kelling Heath Siding

S.B.

An officer's leave ticket issued at Weybourne. *Collection J.M. Strange*

Mid & G. N. Jt. Comm.	Mid & G. N. Jt. Comm.
FURLOUGH	**FURLOUGH**
	Weybourne
to	to
WEYBOURNE	
Via	Via
Available for three months from date of issue	Available for three months from date of issue
FIRST	**FIRST**
For conditions see back	For conditions see back

Fur. Rtn. 2588

other hand, M & GN employees were said to have been remarkably loyal, and one suspects that country station masters such as Mr Whistler were more than happy with their idyllic rural lifestyle!

Weybourne

Departing from Holt, eastbound trains continued north-eastwards for about 1 mile. Holt itself was situated about a quarter of a mile to the north of the railway, but cuttings prevented a clear view of this pleasant Norfolk town. Curving onto a northerly alignment, the route passed under the A148 road, beyond which trains ran through a small copse. After about three quarters of a mile the line ran past the site of Kelling sidings; opened in 1901, these formerly gave access to extensive sand and gravel pits that had supplied the raw materials for the M & GN's characteristic concrete signal and mile posts.

The sidings were 6 miles 69 chains from Melton Constable, at (or very near) the point at which the abortive Blakeney branch would have diverged from the main Cromer route. They were worked by an occupation key system whereby freight trains could be safely 'locked' clear of the running line while passenger workings occupied the Holt–Weybourne single line section.

After traversing Kelling Heath, the railway plunged into a further stretch of cuttings and, turning due east, down trains passed Hundred Acre Wood before they rumbled across a small stream known as Weybourne Spring. The brick-arched underbridge provided at this point had a single clear span of 30 ft. Beyond, trains passed beneath a triple-arched brick overbridge and then came to a stand in the 350 ft long down platform at Weybourne.

One of the most attractive stations on the entire Midland & Great Northern system, Weybourne was 8 miles 55 chains from Melton Constable. A passing place, it had up and down platforms, the main station building being on the down side of the line. Two dead-end goods sidings were also available, but no goods shed was provided at this somewhat remote place; the passing loop was 400 yards long.

Architecturally, Weybourne's surprisingly well-built station buildings did not exhibit any particular style; there were no overtly gothic or classical details, and like most M & GN stations, Weybourne was a *tour de force* of purely late Victorian architecture – an essay in Norman Shaw-style modernity that had allowed local craftsmen and bricklayers to display their skills in the use of brickwork and other contemporary materials. The building was built to the familiar 'hall-and-cross-wings' plan with a centrally-placed booking hall flanked by two gabled cross-wings. The platform frontage was protected by a projecting wooden canopy with traditional saw-tooth valancing, and the roof was adorned with a number of ornate finials.

The building was constructed of red brickwork, laid in the usual Flemish bond. Decorative features included copings along the gables and a raised glass 'lantern' above the gentlemen's toilet; the date '1900' was displayed at the rear (this being the date of building rather than the year of opening, which took place in the following year). The rear windows had six large panes, whereas those facing the platform had only four. Internally, there was room for comparatively lavish accommodation for both staff and passengers, and Major Druitt's 1901 inspection report refers to the usual booking office and waiting room facilities, together with a ladies' room, male and female toilets, a parcels room and a station master's office.

Facilities on the up side were more primitive, the only accommodation for travellers being a small brick-built waiting shelter of typical Midland & Great Northern design. The only other building on the up platform was a single-storey signal cabin. Minor details at this attractive country station included the usual Midland & Great Northern style diagonal fencing, which was similar (though not identical) to Midland-type platform fencing and underlined the close links between the M&GN and its allies at Derby.

Weybourne's first permanent station master was probably Mr S.A. Unwin, who was known to have worked in the station in 1903–4. A few years later, in 1908, the station master was Samuel Bull; Mr Bull had served at several other Midland & Great Northern stations – indeed, his career had started before the formation of the M&GN, and he had earlier worked for the Eastern & Midlands Railway as station master at nearby Sheringham. Samuel Bull was still in charge at Weybourne around 1912–14, but he had evidently left the station by the 1920s. One of his immediate successors was Arthur Youngman, who supervised Weybourne station around 1921–26.

Weybourne never developed as a holiday resort, and in retrospect one suspects that the transport needs of local villagers could easily have been satisfied by a smaller, simpler station. One impediment to the growth of the village was its relatively long distance from the railway – after all, potential holidaymakers do not normally relish the prospect of carrying heavy luggage for any great distance. On the other hand, Weybourne station was conveniently-sited in relation to nearby army facilities at Stiffkey and Weybourne and, until the closure of these camps in the 1950s, the station was regularly used by contingents of soldiers travelling to or from the two camps.

The road from Weybourne Heath to Weybourne village crossed the line on the substantial, triple-arched overbridge at the western end of the station, though the village itself was about 1 mile from the railway – the station being situated in entirely rural surroundings. Indeed, the immediate locality was unusually picturesque, with a well-wooded ridge to the south and the iron-grey waters of the North Sea just 1½ miles to the north.

Sheringham

From Weybourne, the single line swung north-eastwards in a great arc, and, having passed through a deep cutting, trains dropped towards the sea on gradients as steep as 1 in 80. With wooded hills still visible to the right, the line crossed the A149 road on a single span girder bridge before the route turned onto an easterly heading. Running through another cutting, the line passed beneath an overbridge, beyond which the route ran parallel to the sea; to the right, the A149 pursued a corresponding course, while to the left open fields gave way to breezy golf links as the railway neared the important intermediate station at Sheringham.

Having reached an elevation of around 50 ft above mean sea level, the route undulated as it approached Sheringham, the station itself being situ-

An early view of Weybourne station, looking west towards Melton Constable. The single-storey signal cabin enabled signalmen to obtain a clear view through the bridge arch. *Oakwood Collection*

The station buildings at Weybourne station now the temporary western terminus of the preserved line of the North Norfolk Railway. *Author*

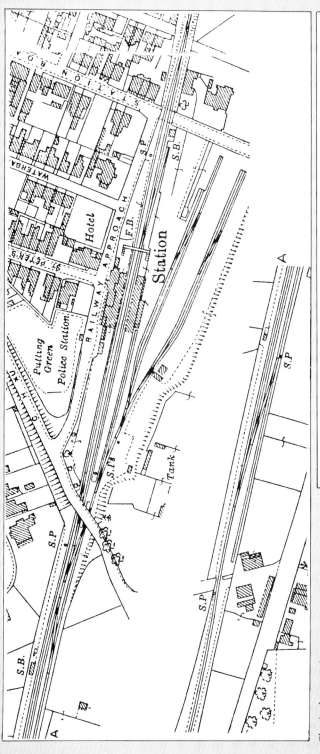

Sheringham station.

Reproduced from 1928, 25" Ordnance Survey map

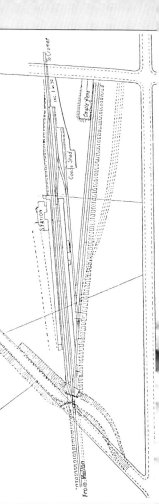

SHERINGHAM STATION YARD.

The contractor's drawing of Sheringham station in 1887.

ated on a 1 in 330 falling gradient. Serving a popular seaside town, Sheringham was 11 miles 30 chains from Melton Constable, and in terms of passenger traffic it was the most important station on the M&GN Cromer branch.
The town was primarily a railway creation, and its development would not
have been possible without the presence of the Midland & Great Northern
line – which brought large numbers of summer visitors from Leicester,
Nottingham and elsewhere.

Sheringham station reflected the town's status as a significant holiday
destination. The layout provided three long platform faces, one of which
was a dead-end bay while the remaining two were through platforms. The
station had originally been a simple two-platform stopping place, but a
series of improvements carried out in 1896–7 and 1904–06 resulted in a
much enlarged station with a 770 yds-long crossing loop and spacious
platforms.[13] In its enlarged form the station had five long sidings together
with a goods loop and a lengthy headshunt on the up side; incoming
excursions were sometimes stabled in the bay platform, but when traffic was
especially heavy spare coaching stock was also parked in the adjacent goods
sidings.

The main station building was on the down side, and there were also a
large building on the up platform, both buildings being solidly built of brick.
Extensive, glass-covered canopies were provided on both the up and down
sides of the station, and the two platforms were physically linked by a lattice
girder footbridge.

A small brick building on the down side was used by Great Eastern staff –
Sheringham being used as a 'terminus' by GER services which (after 1906)
were able to run through to the resort via Cromer Junction and Newstead
Lane Junction. The Great Eastern Company stationed two drivers and two
firemen at Sheringham for working its through express services to London,
but apart from a mess room and an engine inspection pit there were no other
facilities for GER locomotives or train crews.

· Although Sheringham was an important passenger station it handled only
modest amounts of goods traffic. In the early days there had been considerable traffic in bricks, timber and other building materials, but this traffic
became less important once the new resort of Sheringham was fully developed; thereafter, domestic coal supplies ensured that the spacious goods
yard handled at least one form of bulk traffic – though it was significant that
no goods shed was ever needed, and most loading or unloading operations
took place in an open loading dock (part of which was used as a cattle dock).

In its original guise Sheringham station had been controlled from another
unusually-tall signal cabin on the up platform, the level crossing at the
eastern end of the platforms being (presumably) worked by a gateman. These
arrangements were superceded in the early 1900s when the M&GN resignal-
led the station; the old (14-lever) box was abolished and in its place 'East'
and 'West' cabins were erected, the new facilities being inspected in July
1906. The new boxes were strategically-sited at each end of the crossing
loop, the East box being conveniently-close to the busy level crossing at 11
miles 38 chains.[14]

Sheringham station, seen from the nearby road overbridge c.1912. Note that, in the absence of proper carriage sidings, spare coaching stock has been shunted into the goods yard. *Real Photographs*

Sheringham station, looking west towards Melton Constable in the Edwardian era; in the left distance, passenger stock can be seen in the goods yard – there being no proper carriage sidings at this busy seaside station. *Lens of Sutton*

Johnson class 'C' 4-4-0 No. 51 seen here with a rebuilt larger boiler, Deeley cab and Belpaire firebox. The engine is here running tender-first in this 1935 view at Sheringham.

Lens of Sutton

The large overbridge at the west-end of Sheringham station was built at the turn of the century, when the layout here was extensively remodelled.

Lens of Sutton

Beyer, Peacock class 'A' 4-4-0 No. 31 stands in the platform at Sheringham with a Cromer train. This engine was built in 1886 (as works No. 2798) and withdrawn by the M&GNR in 1933.

Loco. Publishing Co.

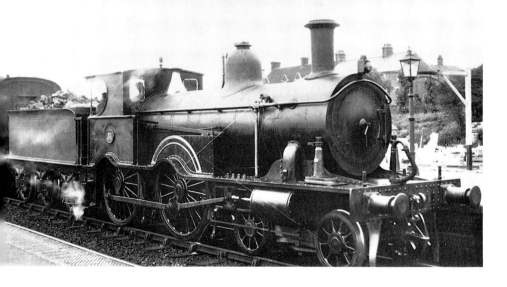

A general view of Sheringham station in 1959. *Lens of Sutton*

A view along the line between Sheringham and West Runton. *H.N. James*

Former Great Northe[r]n locomotives were used [on] the line in increasi[ng] numbers during the la[te] LNER era; here, ex-G[N] 4–4–0 No. 3042 stan[ds] in the westbound pl[at]form at Sheringham [on] 21st August, 1946.
R.M. Casserl[ey]

The M & G N R 4 – 4 – 0s were employed on freight workings as well as on passenger duties and the 1920s view portrays class 'C' 4 – 4 – 0 No. 1 at the head of a down goods train at Sheringham. The formation includes four vans, four cattle wagons and at least eleven open wagons.

Real Photographs

Minor details at Sheringham included some typical Midland & Great Northern-style somersault signals, many of which were mounted on concrete posts. The up starting signal at the western end of the up platform was a particularly good specimen; this signal incorporated a subsidiary siding arm to control access to the goods loop beyond the nearby road overbridge. Water columns were provided on the up and down platforms, and at night the station was illuminated by gas (later by electricity).

The 1888 *Kelly's Directory of Norfolk* records that Sheringham station was supervised by station master Samuel Bull, who later moved to Weybourne. In 1896 the local station master was Frank Rice, and he continued in office for around 30 years. Like many M&GN staff, Mr Rice was always courteous and helpful to the travelling public, and William Marriott mentioned that he was sometimes asked if 'that nice station master' was still at Sheringham? (Writing in 1920/21 he added that he *was* still there!) Frank Rice had, however, retired a short time later, one of his immediate successors being Lionel H. Brooke who was in charge of the station during the early 1920s.

Pulling away from Sheringham's down platform, Cromer trains glided over busy Station Road on the level and, gathering speed, locomotives then tackled a 1 in 264 rising gradient. Reaching a stretch of embankment the route continued parallel to the A149 Cromer Road, and with Sheringham visible to the left trains rumbled over Beeston Road on an overbridge.

As their trains proceeded eastwards travellers could, by glancing to the south, discern a ruined Augustinian Priory standing in fields beside a farm; to the north, Beeston Regis church could be reached by means of a lonely track that crossed the railway on the level.

West Runton

With the gradient steepening to 1 in 107, the single line passed beneath the A149 for the second time since leaving Holt, the brick overbridge provided at this point being wide enough to accommodate a second line of rails (though the line was always single track). West Runton, 13 miles 7 chains, was only a short distance further on. The smallest station on the Melton Constable to Cromer branch, West Runton had just one platform on the up side of the line. This tiny, intermediate stopping place was equipped with a simple wooden station building affording only rudimentary facilities for the travelling public. In Edwardian days, a grounded van body had functioned as a makeshift store for parcels and other small consignments, but this facility was later removed, a small corrugated iron hut being erected in its place.

No sidings or other connections were ever provided here, and the station was, in effect, little more than a halt. The surrounding coastal scenery was, on the other hand, attractive to increasing numbers of holidaymakers, and West Runton eventually developed as a small, but busy resort in its own right. (In the 1950s West Runton enjoyed a good summer train service, and as we shall see, this tiny station was ultimately served by both the 'Broadsman' and the 'Norfolkman' expresses!)

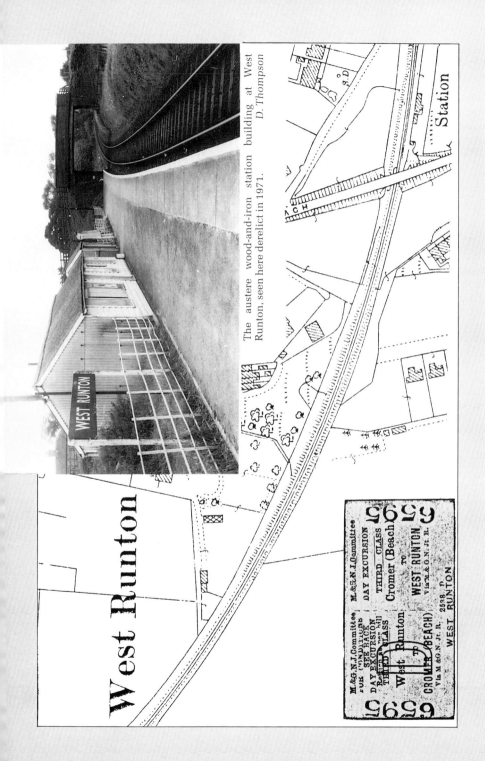

West Runton

The austere wood-and-iron station building at West Runton, seen here derelict in 1971.
D. Thompson

Station

West Runton station, probably photographed during the early 1920s. There was sufficient space here for a second platform, if traffic had justified such a facility.

Lens of Sutton

Another early view of West Runton station with its simple style building. *J. Kite*

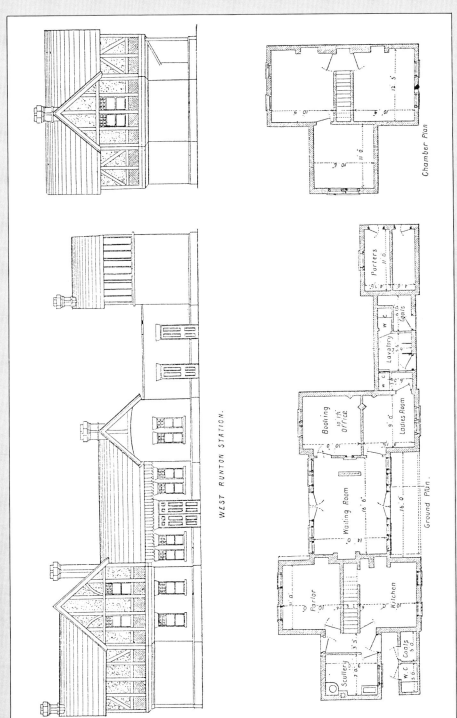

WEST RUNTON STATION.

Chamber Plan

Ground Plan

Booking Office

Waiting Room

Ladies Room

Parlor

Kitchen

Scullery

Porters

Lavatory

Coals

Coals

W.C.

W.C.

A large station was originally planned at West Runton, but in the event the substantial buildings shown in this 1887 contractor's plan were never erected, and the station remained little more than a staffed halt!

Although only a small place, West Runton was evidently considered important enough to have its own station master, and this office was filled, during the 1880s, by a Mr Copland. In 1908 the station master was Benjamin Stone, and he was followed, around 1912, by Robert King; a later station master was William Bunting, who was in charge during the early 1920s.

From West Runton the branch continued east towards its destination, but before entering Cromer the line became double at Runton West Junction (13 miles 65 chains). Opened in 1906, Runton West Junction was situated at the western end of the triangular junction by means of which the Norfolk & Suffolk Joint line left the M&GN route. The junction was controlled from an ornate, Great Northern-style signal cabin on the down side, a similar cabin being provided at Runton East Junction, where the south-to-east curve from Newstead Lane Junction converged with the original M&GN route.

Taking the left hand line, Cromer trains ran through a shallow cutting while, to the right, the double track spur to Newstead Lane Junction continued parallel to the Cromer line for a short distance before veering away to the right; there were, as a result, no less than four lines at this point, and uninitiated travellers were no doubt surprised to discover a quadruple-track railway in this remote place! Soon, however, the diverging routes parted company, and running on their own embankments both lines passed over a minor road on arched viaducts, the M&GN bridge having three spans while its near-neighbour on the Norfolk & Suffolk Joint line was a five-span structure.

Runton East Junction was just 54 chains from Runton West, the line between these two places being worked as a conventional double track section. Runton East Junction Box also controlled the private siding connection to Cromer Gas Works; this facility was situated on the up side of the line.

Cromer Beach

Entering a deep cutting, the line curved gradually north-eastwards, and having passed beneath an overbridge, trains emerged from the cutting and entered the long, main platform at Cromer Beach station (15 miles 16 chains). Passenger facilities here were relatively lavish, though, as mentioned above, there was only one main platform and a short bay. The main platform had run-round facilities, and there was an array of parallel carriage sidings to the north-west. Other sidings branched out to serve the adjacent goods yard, and there was also a single-road engine shed and a 65 ft diameter turntable.

Cromer's basic track layout remained more or less unchanged until the 1950s, although small alterations were effected from time to time. In the Edwardian period, for example, access to the goods yard and carriage sidings had been by means of a somewhat complicated double slip arrangement, but this complex piece of pointwork was later eliminated. Other changes concerned the station's run-round facilities, which had originally provided separate passenger and goods arrival lines alongside the main passenger platform; early maps show that there were two crossovers at the northernmost extremity on the platform – one enabling incoming passenger

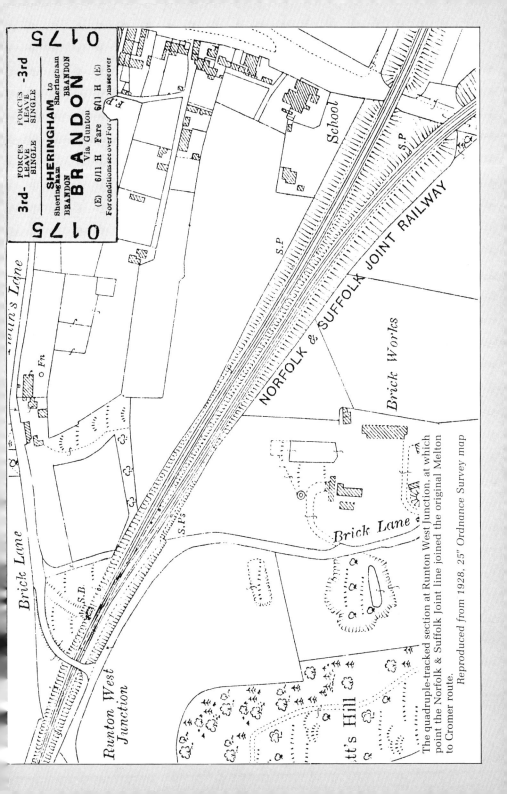

The quadruple-tracked section at Runton West Junction, at which point the Norfolk & Suffolk Joint line joined the original Melton to Cromer route.

Reproduced from 1928, 25″ Ordnance Survey map

NORFOLK & SUFFOLK JOINT RAILWAY

Runton West Junction

Brick Lane

Brick Lane

Brick Works

School

S.P.

S.P.

S.P.

S.P.

S.B.

○ Fn

'tt's Hill

A fine early view of a 10-coach train coming off the Norfolk and Suffolk Joint line at Runton West Junction. The locomotive has a destination board marked 'OVERSTRAND'. Note the signal man offering the token from the specially built platform. *LRGP*

The timber framed signal cabin at Runton West Junction was, like many others on the M&GN system, of Great Northern design. The token exchange platform is smaller than in the previous picture. *H.N. James*

A class '31' A1A-A1A stands on the N&SJ line at Runton West Junction; a typical Marriott-designed overbridge can be glimpsed in the background. *H.N. James*

trains to be run-round while the other (linking the engine release road to an adjacent siding) acted as a subsidiary run-round for use when goods trains or empty stock workings arrived at busy periods. The GER 'system map' dated 25th December, 1919 reveals that the two crossovers were still *in situ* at that time, but the subsidiary connection was subsequently removed, and thereafter what had hitherto been the outer loop became a simple dead-end siding entered from the Melton end of the station.

The main station building was a large and complex structure providing a variety of facilities for the travelling public. The building was seen to advantage from the station approach road, which climbed up to platform level from nearby Holt Road. Walking up this gently-sloping approach, travellers saw in front of them a large two-storey wing with twin gables at right angles to the platform; a large sign revealed that this part of the building was used as a refreshment room. The lower storey was a conventional brick-built structure with large-paned, square-headed windows, while the upper floor was finished in a curious 'timber framed Tudor' style, its lower panels being filled with 'herring bone' brickwork. The upper floor was jetted-out beyond the limits of the lower-storey and this feature added to the 'Tudor' effect.

A centrally-placed booking hall was arranged at right angles to the two-storied eastern wing, and this part of the building incorporated a projecting *porte-cochère* with ornate metal spandrels bearing the initials 'M & GN'. The overall appearance of this fine station reflected the Arts and Crafts movement that had been in vogue around the time of its construction.

Looking beyond the central block, travellers with an interest in railway architecture may have noticed that although there was another cross wing at the far end of the building, the westernmost wing did not match the one at the eastern end of the station, and whereas the east wing was a two-gabled structure its counterpart at the Sheringham end of the building had just one roof ridge. Moreover, the west wing was longer than the 'refreshment room' wing, and for this reason the station building had an 'L'-shaped ground plan, the western wing constituting the bottom stroke of the 'L'. Like the 'refreshment room' block, the western wing was of two full stories, though the intervening booking hall was a single-storey structure.

The main platform was covered by a train shed, the latter facility being an integral part of the station building. The train shed was supported, on one side, by a substantial brick wall and on the other by the station building; transverse girders extended across the platform between the station building and the supporting wall, and the train shed featured a 14-bay 'ridge and furrow' type roof. Glazed screens were provided at the eastern (i.e. seaward) end of the train shed but the opposite end was open to the elements; the train shed was 176 ft 3 in. long, and it therefore covered the first three coaches of an incoming train.

On a footnote, it is interesting to note that the metal spandrels on the platform side of the train shed sported the initials 'E & MR' – suggesting that the porch (with its M & GN ironwork) had been added after the formation of the Midland & Great Northern organisation in 1893.

An early view of Cromer Beach station, looking towards the terminal buffer stops. Note the original flat-bottomed trackwork (left) and the low, single-storey block in the foreground – which differs considerably in relation to Marriott's original plans.

Oakwood Collection

A detailed view of the eastern end of Cromer Beach station, showing the overall roof and part of the refreshment room block. *Lens of Sutton*

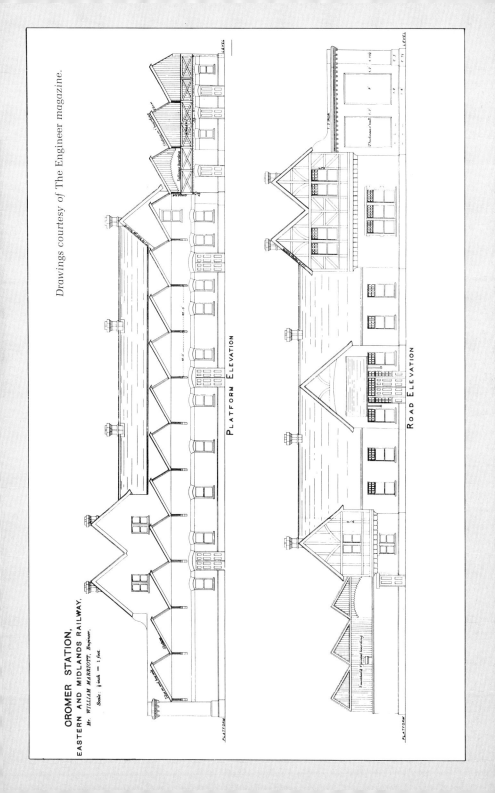

Drawings courtesy of The Engineer magazine.

CROMER STATION,
EASTERN AND MIDLANDS RAILWAY.
Mr. WILLIAM MARRIOTT, Engineer.
Scale: ⅛ inch = 1 foot.

PLATFORM ELEVATION

ROAD ELEVATION

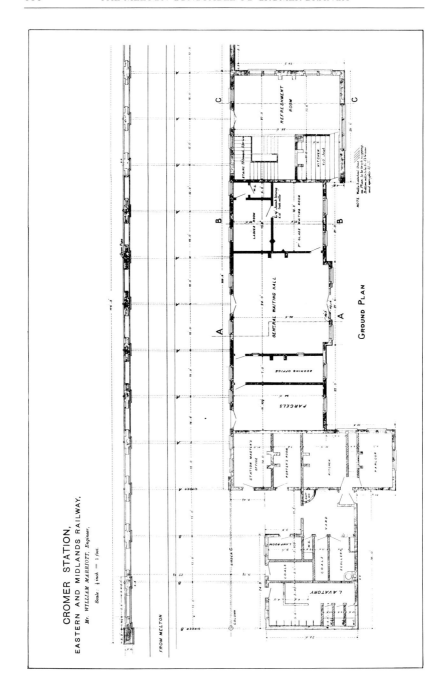

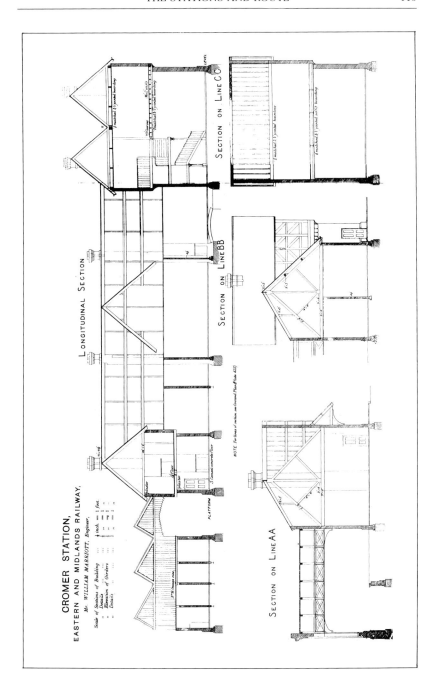

CROMER STATION,
EASTERN AND MIDLANDS RAILWAY,
Mr. WILLIAM MARRIOTT, Engineer,

A rear view of Cromer Beach station, showing the refreshment room wing (*right*) and the slightly longer station master's wing (*middle distance*).   *Real Photographs*

A rare view showing the interior of the train shed with useful detail of the transverse girders which supported Marriott's ridge-and-furrow roof.   *Lens of Sutton*

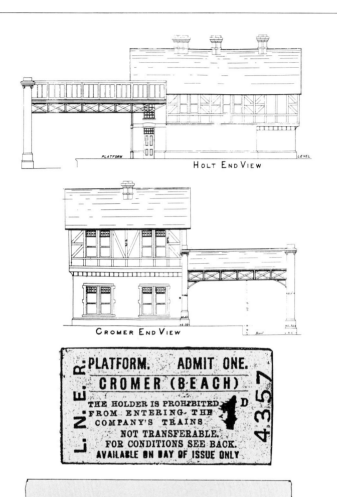

HOLT END VIEW

CROMER END VIEW

PLATFORM. ADMIT ONE.
CROMER (BEACH)
THE HOLDER IS PROHIBITED
FROM ENTERING THE
COMPANY'S TRAINS
NOT TRANSFERABLE.
FOR CONDITIONS SEE BACK.
AVAILABLE ON DAY OF ISSUE ONLY

(18—V19)
MIDLAND & GREAT NORTHERN RAILWAYS
JOINT COMMITTEE.

TO
Cromer Beach

Class 'B1' 4–6–0 No. 61113 stands in the main platform at Cromer Beach with an enthusiasts' excursion on 19th September, 1954.   *H.C. Casserley*

A Metro-Cammell class '101' multiple unit departs from Cromer Beach on the last leg of its journey from Norwich to Sheringham. (The signal cabin incorporates concrete components fabricated in the M&GN works at Melton Constable.) Note the tablet catchers, and the deep cuttings beyond the dmu.   *Author*

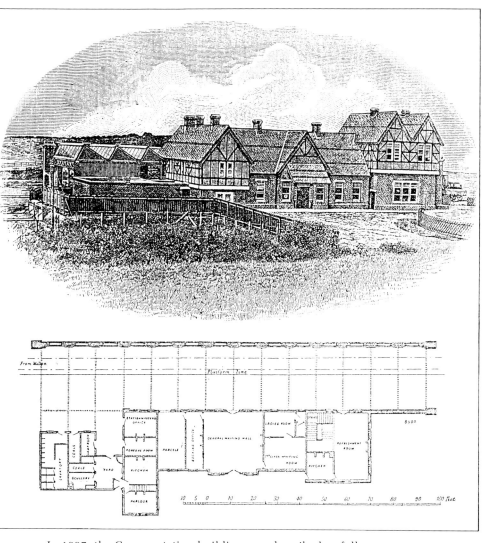

In 1887, the Cromer station building was described as follows:

This station has a covered platform 175 ft long, the roofing being framed as shown in the sketch, so that the glass is nearly vertical. The arrangement of the building is shown on the plan, and the accommodation, though small, is very complete. It comprises a hall 26 ft square, a first class waiting room 18 ft by 13 ft 6 in., a ladies' room 14 ft by 10 ft, a booking-office 24 ft by 7 ft, a parcels office 24 ft by 12 ft, station master's office 14 ft by 10 ft, and porters' room 14 ft by 7 ft. There is also a good-sized refreshment room with kitchen and necessary offices. Above the ground floor, which is 12 ft high, at one end of the station building are the rooms occupied by the station master. As will be seen from our perspective view the general design of the building is very good.

Extract from the 1887 Engineering magazine

A fascinating early view of Cromer Beach showing a profusion of flat-bottomed trackwork and the unusual brick-built water tower (*left*).   *Oakwood Collection*

A more recent view of the terminal buildings at Cromer Beach, now like other station buildings on the Norwich to Sheringham line, merely an unstaffed halt.

Lens of Sutton

Like other large, and relatively complex structures, Cromer Beach station was modified in various small ways throughout its long career. It is, nonetheless, interesting to examine the internal layout of this 'vernacular revival' building as it would have appeared in its Edwardian heyday, and in this respect, we are fortunate in that the *Railway Engineer* published a detailed set of plans of the station in January 1890.

The plans, which emanated from William Marriott's own office, provide an insight into the type of passenger accommodation that was considered necessary during the late-Victorian era. There was full provision for all classes of traveller, first class customers and ladies being afforded the luxury of separate waiting room facilities while (in an age when middle class travellers invariably packed their belongings into voluminous luggage) there were ample porters' rooms and parcels accommodation.

The notes which follow will describe the internal arrangements as they were in the 1890s, though it should be stressed that the layout of the building was changed in later years – albeit in minor ways.

Internally, Cromer station building incorporated the usual booking office and waiting room facilities, together with suitable domestic accommodation for the station master and his family. Entering the building through double doors at the rear, travellers immediately entered the commodious waiting room-cum-booking hall which occupied the entire width of the central block. To the right, internal doors gave access to a first class waiting room, while to the left a similar doorway enabled staff to enter the ticket office. The booking hall measured approximately 26 ft × 26 ft at ground floor level, and the adjacent ticket office measured 26 ft × 7 ft. The first class waiting room was linked to a smaller room which functioned as a ladies' waiting room, while the ticket office was conveniently close to a parcels office; the booking hall and parcels office were both provided with double doors on the platform side of the building, but there was no means of direct access from the platform to the ticket office or the first class waiting room.

Another pair of double doors led from the platform to the refreshment room, which, like the booking hall, was a large room spanning the entire width of the building. The overall dimensions of the refreshment room wing were approximately 29 ft × 30 ft at ground level (the jetted upper storey being slightly larger).

The western wing was primarily a domestic block, and its ground floor contained four relatively small rooms which were (from front to back) a station master's office, a porters' room, the station master's kitchen, and a domestic parlour. A staircase ascended to the upper storey between the kitchen and parlour, and this gave access to bedrooms, etc., used by the station master's family. There was, in addition, a cluster of stores and outhouses at the extreme western end of the station building, and these provided public toilet facilities and extra storage capacity for coal, lamps and other items; part of this area served as a scullery and yard for the station master's domestic use.

One small point of detail that might be mentioned concerns the roof construction method used above the central booking hall block. A glance at the plans (reproduced on another page) will reveal that the booking hall roof

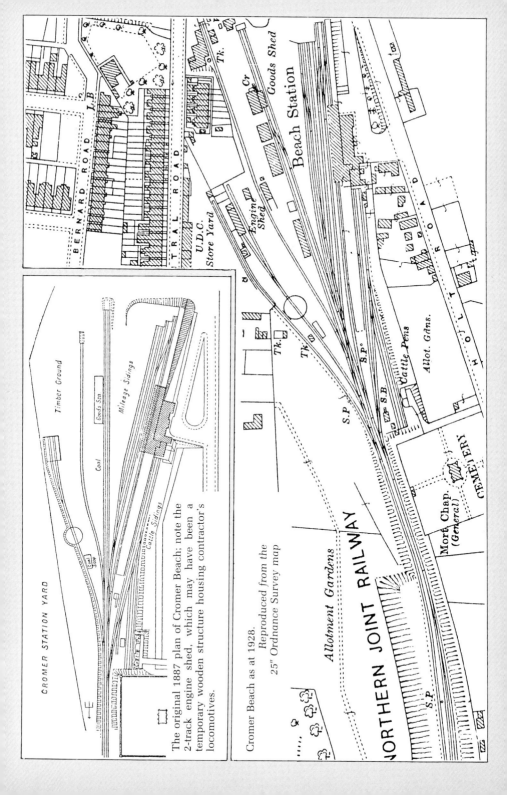

CROMER STATION YARD

Timber Ground

Goods Stn

Coal

Mileage Sidings

Cattle Sidings

The original 1887 plan of Cromer Beach; note the 2-track engine shed, which may have been a temporary wooden structure housing contractor's locomotives.

Cromer Beach as at 1928.
Reproduced from the
25" Ordnance Survey map

BERNARD ROAD

L.B

CENTRAL ROAD

U.D.C.
Store Yard

Tk.

Cr

Engine
Shed

Goods Shed

Beach Station

Tk.

Tk.

S.P°

S.B

Cattle Pens

Allot. Gdns.

HOLT ROAD

S.P°

S.P.

S.P.

Mort. Chap.
(General)

CEMETERY

Allotment Gardens

NORTHERN JOINT RAILWAY

was asymmetric, but a conventional tie beam and king post assembly was nevertheless employed to form a sort of sub-structure which, in turn, provided a firm basis for the common rafters. Ordinary purlins were used on the road side of the station, but rafters on the platform side were supported by a row of vertical struts resting on the internal sub-structure; the weight of these struts was transmitted to the tie beams by means of 4 in. × 4 in. diagonal struts linking the king posts to the principal rafters.

Cromer was the only station on the branch from Melton Constable to have a proper goods shed, this brick-built structure being sited beside one of the three long goods sidings to the north of the passenger station. Other buildings in the goods yard included a goods office at the eastern end of the yard and a stable block. There were in addition a number of small sheds that were used as stores or offices by local coal merchants, and these sheds were, for the most part, simple gable-roofed buildings of no architectural pretention.

The three goods sidings were between 660 and 700 ft long, that on the northern side of the yard being 40 ft shorter than the two southernmost goods roads; the latter were linked by a crossover to form a run-round loop for use during shunting operations.

Cromer's locomotive facilities were situated on the north-west side of the station complex. There were several sidings, one of them serving the 65 ft diameter turntable while another was used as an ash wagon road. The engine shed was situated at the end of another siding, and an adjacent spur provided additional storage space for locomotives. The shed itself was a conventional brick structure with a length of approximately 60 ft; it had four, slightly-arched windows on either side, and there was a very low clerestorey along the apex of the roof. An ash pit and coaling facilities were available at one end of the locomotive yard, and there was, at one time, a small, brick-built water tower with a curious pitched roof over its metal tank.

The private siding serving the Cromer Electricity Supply Works was situated at the rear of the engine shed, the total length of this siding being 600 ft; the electricity supply siding was protected by a gate where it left railway property and entered the electricity works.

In common with Holt and Sheringham, Cromer Beach once boasted an unusually-tall wooden signal cabin. Sited near the western end of the platform, this towering structure was three stories high, and its glazed upper floor enabled signalmen to obtain an excellent bird's eye view over the entire station and its approaches. The original (20-lever) box was later demolished, a two-storey cabin being erected in its place; the new box – which originally had 29 levers – was of traditional appearance with a hipped roof and small-paned window frames. (An enlarged 35 lever frame was later installed.)

The terminus was signalled in such a way that incoming trains could enter either platform or the goods yard – a bracket signal with three 'home' arms being provided at the station throat. In the reverse direction, a two-doll starting signal at the end of the platform allowed both platform roads to be used for departures as well as arriving trains. At the end of the 19th century the starting signals had been of the slotted-post variety, but characteristic

M&GN 'somersault' signals had been installed by the turn-of-the-century. The station was lit by gas, and ornate lamp posts were provided along the length of the platform. These were of an unusual design with posts formed of a series of tubes of differing diameter – the bottom part being thicker than the upper parts so that the lamp posts looked rather like extended tele-scopes; each tubular section was joined to its neighbours by a bulging 'knop', and the glass lanterns tapered towards the base. Other platform furniture at Cromer Beach included the usual M&GN diagonal fencing, while the name 'CROMER BEACH' was displayed on large wooden name-boards with raised letters.

The railways were, in former times, significant employers in the Cromer area. The M&GN and Great Eastern companies maintained separate staffing establishments, the town's two terminal stations each having their own station masters, booking clerks, porters, signalmen, goods staff, locomotive crews and permanent way gangs. Cromer Beach was, in the M&GN terms, an important terminus, and its station master was a figure of some authority; one of the longest-serving station masters here was Seth Bastow, who was in office during the Edwardian period, and throughout World War I. Mr Bastow came to Cromer during the 1890s, having already served as station master at Melton Constable; his predecessor at Cromer – Mr Whistler – subsequently moved to Holt.

Cromer itself could easily be reached from the M&GN station, and travellers who, on leaving the terminus, walked down West Street, soon found themselves in the centre of the historic town. The beach, with its picturesque fishing vessels, was only a short distance further on, while lofty cliffs rose impressively on either side. Those with an interest in railways may have been tempted to trek out to the southern outskirts of the town in order to see the rival GER terminus – an interesting feature of the Great Eastern station being the 61 yds-long tunnel which enabled the Norfolk & Suffolk Joint line to pass beneath the GER on its way from Runton West Junction to Mundesley; this short bore was one of only two tunnels in Norfolk. (The other was at Barsham on the Wells-next-the-Sea branch.)

Like Sheringham, Cromer was, above all, a railway creation that simply would not have existed if the railways had not been able to transport large numbers of people to and from the coast. In pre-railway days it had been merely a village, but the opening of the East Norfolk line in 1877 trans-formed Cromer into a small, but busy residential and holiday centre.

Apart from a small nucleus of narrow, Medieval streets around the Parish Church, the town was of predominantly Victorian appearance, with many large red brick hotels – most of them within easy walking distance of Cromer Beach station. The largest of these late 19th century 'palaces' was the Grand Hotel, on West Cliff; built by local architect George Skipper (1856–1948) it was opened in 1891, and could accommodate 150 guests. The Hotel de Paris and the Metropole Hotel were of equal magnificence. Both were designed by Skipper on a lavish scale; the Hotel de Paris – in a dominant position above the pier – was built on the 'sun-trap' principle, with an angled facade to catch the rays of the morning or evening sun.

It is interesting to note that most of Cromer's red brick hotels and guest houses were built in a somewhat similar architectural style that owned much to the so-called 'vernacular revival'. Although not as ornate as some of the earlier Victorian building styles, these turn-of-the-century villas and guest houses featured a variety of vaguely-Jacobean details such as mullion windows and prominent gables. The stations at Holt, Weybourne, Sheringham and Cromer Beach shared many of these attributes, and discerning visitors – or those with an eye for architectural minutiae – would have realised that the Melton to Cromer line was a reflection of Cromer itself. The railway, and the resort that it helped bring into existence, were built in a particular place at a particular time, and it is perhaps hardly surprising that the red brick architecture of the Midland & Great Northern Joint Railway so closely matched that of the surrounding area.

'D' class 0–6–0 No. 59 (as LNER No. 059) heads a local passenger train at Cromer Beach around 1939; this engine was built by Neilson in 1896 (with No. 5033) and withdrawn in 1944.   H.C. Casserley

Marriott 4–4–2T No. 20 stands in the bay platform at Cromer Beach. The vehicle on the left is a former Lancashire & Yorkshire coach that has presumably worked through from Lancashire on a special. The year is 1929.   H.C. Casserley

Johnson class 'C' 4–4–0 No. 1 backs out of the bay platform at Cromer Beach with a train of ex-GNR four-wheelers on 26th June, 1929. There was no run-round track in this bay and incoming trains had to reverse out of the platform in order to run-round on the main loop.   *H.C. Casserley*

A striking portrait of a Beyer, Peacock class 'A' 4–4–0 No. 32 outside the three-road engine shed at Melton Constable. A class 'C' 4–4–0 lurks in the background. The class 'A' worked for many years on the Cromer branch.   *Loco. Publishing Co.*

Chapter Six
The Post-War Years (1948–1989)

The end of the war in Europe had been followed, in July 1945, by the election of a new, and radical Labour government. This incoming administration was pledged to bring railways, mines and other important industries into public ownership, and as far as railways were concerned, 'nationalisation' was put into effect at midnight on 31st December, 1947. A new organisation, known as British Railways, replaced the 'Big Four' private companies, although it soon became apparent that a large measure of regional autonomy would be retained; the former GER and M&GN systems, for instance, became part of the 'Eastern Region' of British Railways, and this geographically-defined region retained many pre-nationalisation (and even pre-grouping) features.

Post-War Changes at Cromer

In retrospect, the creation of British Railways did not entail any immediate changes – the one obvious alteration carried out after 1948 being the application of new liveries for locomotives and rolling stock. The varnished teak or middle-brown liveries that had traditionally been carried by LNER group coaching stock was replaced by a striking red and cream colour scheme that did much to brighten the 'austerity' image of post-war Britain, while non-corridor vehicles were painted in an overall maroon livery that was, in effect, a reversion to the style of painting favoured by the Midland Railway (and indeed the GER for a short period during the early 1900s). Locomotives, meanwhile, were painted in a range of liveries – though most of the classes seen on the lines to Cromer appeared in unadorned black.

Apart from these livery changes (which took many months to implement) the only innovation initiated locally under BR auspices was a logical renaming of the former Great Eastern terminus at Cromer, which henceforth became known as 'Cromer High'; this renaming officially took place in September 1948.

These changes were essentially cosmetic, and no amount of new paintwork or renamings could mask the archaic nature of much of Britain's railway system. Years of under-investment under private ownership had ensured the retention of Edwardian trains and Victorian equipment that should, perhaps, have been replaced at a much earlier date. The locomotives seen in the Cromer area, for example, were of predominantly Great Eastern vintage, the familiar 'Claud Hamilton' 4–4–0s being much in evidence. In 1950, Melton Constable's allocation included Nos. 62509, 62515, 62519, 62520, 62523, 62533, 62538, 62562, 62620 and 62578; some of these (such as Nos. 62509, 62520 and 62538) were small-boilered 'D15's.

Representing an even older generation of motive power, the Worsdell 'J15' 0–6–0s (which worked many local goods services) dated back to the early 1880s, the first member of the class having been introduced in 1883! Stations and other infrastructure were also, for the most part, of 19th century origin, although this was no great disadvantage to the travelling public – Victorian architecture was, after all, built to last, and stations such as Cromer Beach were clearly adequate for the needs of modern passengers.

The early 1950s were, nevertheless, years of modest development in which the anomalies of 19th century competitive capitalism were gradually eliminated, one of the most important innovations being at Cromer where the need for two terminal stations within a mile of each other was rightly questioned. In terms of facilities, the rival stations were equally-matched, both having the usual carriage sidings, goods yards and locomotive facilities. The Great Eastern terminus had three platform faces to Cromer Beach's two, but Cromer High was inconveniently-situated in an elevated position on the eastern edge of the town, whereas Cromer Beach occupied a better site near the historic town centre – the parish church of St Peter & St Paul being just 600 yards from the buffer stops. Furthermore, the M&GN station was conveniently-close to the hotels and boarding houses on West Cliff, the beach itself being only a short distance beyond.

Remodelling at Cromer Beach

Cromer Beach station was accessible from both the west and the south, trains from the M&GN line being able to run straight in to the station, while GER line trains from Norwich could reach the terminus by means of the Norfolk & Suffolk Joint line. Conversely, M&GN trains from the west could not reach Cromer High without an awkward and time-consuming reversal at Cromer Junction, and on balance, Cromer Beach was the obvious choice for future development as the town's one and only railway station. It was, accordingly, decided that Cromer High would be closed to passenger traffic, and that all main line and local trains from Norwich would be routed into the former Midland & Great Northern terminus.

It was necessary, before this change could take place, for BR to carry out a remodelling of the signalling and track layout at Cromer Beach. In the early 1950s the M&GN station handled around 15 trains each way during the summer season, and a similar number were dealt with at the former Great Eastern station; closure of the latter would therefore double the amount of passenger traffic handled at Cromer Beach, and in order to accommodate this extra traffic the passenger platform was extended westwards as far as the signal box, and the station approach lines were doubled. At the same time BR engineers removed all facing lock bars and installed 12 new track circuits, while the down home and up starting signals were given new brackets. Fourteen new ground level shunting signals were provided, and to work the revised track layout the lever frame in Cromer Beach signal box was enlarged from 29 to 35 levers.

Passenger facilities were not overlooked, and as part of the comprehensive remodelling at Cromer Beach BR installed electric lighting throughout the station and carried out further work to improve passenger and parcels facilities.

The rebuilding was completed on 19th September, 1954, and Cromer High was closed to passenger traffic on the following day. Henceforth, Cromer would have just one main terminal station, and in a sense the Midland & Great Northern had scored a minor victory over the rival Great Eastern – the GER terminus being reduced to goods-only status! On the other hand, the concentration of passenger services at Cromer Beach can be seen as the start of the process whereby the Great Eastern route from Norwich became Cromer's only rail link with the rest of BR – a process which ultimately resulted in the present day situation in which the historically-separate M & GN and GER routes are worked as one long branch from Norwich.

Train Services in the 1950s

At a time when few British families had access to a motor vehicle, holiday lines such as the former M & GN and GER Cromer routes carried a heavy summer traffic, and the 1956 public timetables provide a glimpse of these rural rail links working at full capacity to move large numbers of holidaymakers to and from the seaside. The basic weekday train service provided 12 trains each way between Melton Constable and Cromer, together with 14 each way on the GER route between Norwich and Cromer. Some of the Norwich workings ran through to Sheringham or Melton Constable after reversal at Cromer Beach, while longer distance through workings via the M & GN line catered for people wishing to visit Cromer from Birmingham, Leicester, or other parts of the Midlands industrial region.

Cromer was, at this time, served by no less than two named trains. These were the 'Norfolkman' and the 'Broadsman' expresses, both of which worked over the M & GN line to Sheringham. Both trains ran daily, with departures from Liverpool Street at 9.30 am and 3.30 pm respectively. The down 'Norfolkman' reached Cromer Beach at 12.47 pm (1.04 pm on Saturdays) and, after reversal, it departed on the last leg of its journey to Sheringham at 12.56 pm; arrival there was at 1.06 pm, giving an overall journey time of 3 hours 36 minutes. The 'Broadsman' followed some six hours later, and arrived in Sheringham at 7.01 pm, seven minutes being allowed for the reversal at Cromer. In the opposite direction, the up 'Norfolkman' left Sheringham at 4.26 pm, reaching Cromer Beach at 4.35 pm and London by 7.55 pm. The 'Broadsman', meanwhile, remained in Norfolk overnight prior to forming an early morning departure from Sheringham at 6.23 am. The up working reached Cromer at 6.32 am, and it arrived in London at 10.00 am; refreshment car facilities were available throughout on this early morning service. Both expresses called intermediately at West Runton, though some of the small stations between Norwich and Cromer were not served by these prestigious named trains.

Other through London services left Sheringham at 7.40, 8.20 am and 12.26 pm, and there were corresponding down workings from Liverpool Street at 12.30, 1.30 and 5.30 pm. The 7.40 am and 12.26 pm up workings commenced their journeys at Melton Constable, and the 12.30 pm and 5.30 pm down services from London ran through beyond Sheringham to Melton.

On a footnote, it may be worth pointing out that southbound trains from Sheringham to London were regarded as 'up' workings on the GER line, but as the M & GN route to London had been via Melton Constable and Peterborough, trains from Cromer Beach to Melton were also designated up workings; it follows that M & GN trains from Melton or Sheringham to Cromer were *down* workings, and through services such as the 'Norfolkman' were therefore regarded as down trains until they reached Cromer. A similar situation pertained in the northbound direction, in that down trains from

Liverpool Street technically became 'up' workings once they gained former M&GN metals at Cromer Beach.

Although ordinary weekday services were provided on a generous scale, the summer Saturday timetable was clearly the highlight of Cromer branch operations. Through workings were available to a variety of destinations, and the fact that all services now ran to or from Cromer Beach meant that connections between the former GER and M&GN routes were easily accomplished. The following table (based upon the June 1956 timetable) will give readers some idea of the wide range of services offered to local travellers at that time.

Table 4

Summary of summer Saturday departures from Cromer Beach in July 1959

Time	Route	Destination	Notes
6.39 am	GER	Liverpool St	The up 'Broadsman'
7.24 am	GER	Norwich	
7.50 am	MGN	Melton Constable	
7.54 am	GER	Liverpool St	From Melton Constable
8.36 am	GER	Liverpool St	From Sheringham
8.40 am	MGN	Birmingham (SO)	Terminated at Melton on weekdays
9.28 am	MGN	Birmingham (SO)	
9.39 am	GER	Liverpool St	From Sheringham (SO)
9.42 am	GER	Sheringham	
10.25 am	GER	Norwich	From Melton Constable
10.34 am	MGN	Melton Constable	
11.39 am	GER	Liverpool St (SO)	From Sheringham
12.17 pm	MGN	Shirebrook West (SO)	
12.30 pm	MGN	Sheringham	Liverpool St
12.34 pm	GER	Liverpool St (SO)	From Melton Constable
1.11 pm	MGN	Sheringham	The down 'Norfolkman'
1.35 pm	MGN	Peterborough Nth (SO)	
1.39 pm	GER	Liverpool St (SO)	From Sheringham
1.50 pm	MGN	Sheringham	From Liverpool St
2.29 pm	MGN	Melton Constable	
3.39 pm	GER	Liverpool St	
3.50 pm	MGN	Leicester (SO)	
4.15 pm	MGN	Melton Constable	Through train from London
4.42 pm	GER	Liverpool St	The up 'Norfolkman'
5.39 pm	GER	Liverpool St	From Sheringham
5.49 pm	MGN	Sheringham	From Liverpool St
6.17 pm	MGN	Melton Constable	
6.48 pm	GER	Norwich	Melton to Norwich
7.00 pm	MGN	Sheringham	The down 'Broadsman'
7.16 pm	GER	Norwich	From Sheringham
7.20 pm	MGN	Melton Constable	Melton to Norwich
9.00 pm	MGN	Norwich	From Melton Constable
9.03 pm	MGN	Melton Constable	Through train from London
10.34 pm	MGN	Melton Constable	

NB The Monday to Friday timetable was similar to that in operation on Saturdays, though some of the 'SO' trains ran at different times.

Study of the above table will show that many of the Norwich or Liverpool Street trains actually started their journeys at Sheringham or Melton Constable, and to that extent the M&GN line was already being worked on a Sheringham–Cromer–Norwich axis; Cromer High may have been closed, but the M&GN Cromer branch was gradually becoming integrated into the rival Great Eastern system.

Sunday services were provided on a comparatively lavish scale during the mid-1950s, and in June 1956 local travellers had a choice of four up and four down trains between Sheringham and Cromer Beach on summer Sundays during the height of the season. Two of the up trains were advertised as 'through trains from Holt to Liverpool Street', while, in the opposite direction, two of the Sunday trains worked through to Holt.

The First Closures

The train services provided during the 1950s were, by normal branch line standards, unusually good, but ironically this excellent service was offered to the public at a time when road transport and government policies were poised to do irreparable harm to the railway industry. It could be argued that some portions of the railway system were never profitable and should not, in fact, have been built; the Cromer to Mundesley line, for example, was a classic 'political' route that failed to realise the high ambitions of its promoters. Needless to say, such lines were particularly vulnerable to road competition, and it is perhaps hardly surprising that the former Norfolk & Suffolk Joint line should have become one of the first post-war closure victims.

The line from Mundesley to Roughton Road Junction was closed on Easter Monday, 6th April, 1953, leaving a residual local service on the southern part of the line between North Walsham and Mundesley-on-Sea. This closure did not affect the northernmost extremity of the N&SJR between Roughton Road Junction and Runton (East and West) Junctions, because this short section of line still formed a vital link between Sheringham and the GER branch to Norwich Thorpe.

The minor closures of the early 1950s can be seen as logical attempts to modernise an irrational railway network that owed more to the whims of competitive Victorian capitalists than the needs of the modern traveller. However, the momentum of closure and retraction, once set in train, soon brought further closures – one of the most spectacular acts of wholesale dismemberment being the slaughter of the Midland & Great Northern main line in 1958. Built to challenge the GER, this east-to-west cross country route was largely duplicated by other lines between Leicester, Birmingham and Norwich; it was, therefore, a potential candidate for closure on crude accountancy grounds, but the basic problem of over-capacity on the routes between East Anglia and the Midlands was compounded by the condition of three large bridges at Cross Keys (over the River Nene), West Lynn (over the Ouse), Potter Heigham (over the River Thurne) and Breydon Water. These were said to be expensive to maintain, while they also imposed weight restrictions on the M&GN route.

In retrospect, the demise of the Midland & Great Northern was inevitable, and the blow finally came on Saturday, 28th February, 1958 when the line was virtually wiped out, leaving the Melton to Cromer branch as a truncated spur that could only be worked as part of the former Great Eastern system. (Other sections were retained for freight traffic – among them the Norwich City line, which could still be reached via Cromer and Melton Constable.)

The Changing Scene

The closure of the M&GN did not, in the short term, have any great impact on the Cromer Beach line. It was true that, for the first time since the 1880s, Cromer and Sheringham lost their direct rail links to the Midlands, but in a sense these did not matter because the branch had already been brought into the main GER system; since 1906, trains from Norwich and Liverpool Street had been able to reach the branch, and this ensured that the former M&GN line slowly became assimilated into the LNER (later Eastern Region) network.

In terms of motive power, the late 1950s and early 1960s were of considerable interest in that a variety of former LNER types were used on the line. Great Eastern types were such in evidence throughout this transition period, but at the same time the appearance of large, modern engines such as 'B1' 4–6–0s, added interest and variety on what had now become the Norwich–Cromer–Melton line.

On a sample day's observation in August 1961, ex-LNER class 'B1' 4–6–0 No. 61043 was seen running tender-first at the head of a Melton Constable to Cromer freight working, while on another occasion 'B1' No. 61283 was seen on a similar local freight working. Another engine noted on these duties was 'Claud Hamilton' 4–4–0 No. 62617, while 'J15' and 'J17' 0–6–0s also appeared on Cromer freight duties.

Passenger workings brought large tank engines such as the 'V3' class 2–6–2Ts or 'A5' 4–6–2Ts onto the line; in 1953, for instance, 'A5/1' class 4–6–2T No. 69826 was seen leaving Sheringham with a four-coach local train. The through Liverpool Street trains could produce anything from a 'V3' 2–6–2T to a 'B1' or 'B17' 4–6–0. To take one example, a *Railway Magazine* correspondent noted that, on a typical day's running in the summer of 1959, the down 'Broadsman' express was brought into Cromer Beach behind class 'B1' 4–6–0 No. 61317; on arrival in the terminus the 'B1' was replaced by 'B17' 4–6–0 No. 61636 *Harlaxton Manor*, which backed on to the train for the remainder of the journey to Sheringham. (A survey of some of the types of motive power seen during the BR era is given in *Table 5*.)

Table 5
CROMER BRANCH MOTIVE POWER c.1930–1966

Type	Wheelbase	Typical Numbers
Worsdell 'J15' class	0–6–0	65373/65390/65417/65469/65479
Holden 'J17' class	0–6–0	
Thompson 'B1' class	4–6–0	61043/61044/61283/61317
Holden 'B12' class	4–6–0	61568
Gresley 'B17' class	4–6–0	61636 Harlaxton Manor
Gresley 'V3' class	2–6–2T	
Robinson 'A5' class	4–6–2T	69826
'Claud Hamilton'	4–4–0	62509/62515/62520/62533/62538/62617
Holden 'F6' class	2–4–2T	67224/67225/67228/67229
Holden 'F3' class	2–4–2T	67152/67162/67178
Fairburn '4MT' class	2–6–4T	
Ivatt '4MT' class	2–6–0	
Gresley 'J39' class*	0–6–0	
Holden 'J67/69' class*	0–6–0T	68536
Holden 'J66' class*	0–6–0T	68377
Hill 'N7' class*	0–6–2T	69679
Gresley 'J6' class*	0–6–0	
Robinson 'J11' class*	0–6–0	
BR class 31	A1A-A1A	
BR class 101	dmu	

NB for completeness, the table includes engines that would have been seen at Melton Constable or on Cromer–Mundesley services; these are distinguised by an asterisk.

Enthusiast's specials were occasionally run during the early 1960s, and on 21st May, 1960 a particularly interesting steam-hauled excursion was organised by the newly-formed Midland & Great Northern Railway Preservation Society. The special, hauled by ex-GER class 'J15' 0–6–0 No. 65469, commenced its journey at Norwich City and, following the closed M&GN branch to Melton Constable, it then traversed the still-extant branch to Cromer Beach before continuing southwards onto the Norwich Thorpe line.

Diesels were first seen on the Melton to Cromer line in the mid-1950s, and as the pace of dieselisation quickened, more and more of the remaining passenger services between Norwich, Cromer Beach and Melton Constable were worked by diesel multiple units. These new trains were, in general, popular among the travelling public – who especially liked the large all-round windows that allowed them to admire the passing scenery. Large main line diesels also appeared on the branch, one of the most characteristic types being the D55XX A1A-A1As (later class '31s') which worked both passenger and freight traffic.

Meanwhile, the rapid dieselisation of the London to Norwich main line had enabled the Eastern Region to introduce a regular interval service between Liverpool Street and Norwich. By the beginning of 1959 the principal workings to and from Norwich were accelerated to provide a two-hour journey time to and from Liverpool Street, but this led, in turn, to a reduction in the amount of through running onto the Cromer and Sheringham line. Most trains between Norwich, Cromer and Melton were now handled by dmu formations, and the 'Broadsman' became the only remaining all-year-round through service between Sheringham and London.

The Beeching Plan

The next few years saw still further retraction in the level of services offered to travellers in the Cromer area, and many local enthusiasts feared that BR intended to close the Melton to Cromer route in its entirety. This unwelcome scenario came much closer in March 1963, when the publication of Dr Richard Beeching's controversial report, entitled The Reshaping of British Railways, recommended the withdrawal of railway passenger services from no less than 5,000 miles of line – among them the section of M&GN line between Melton Constable and Sheringham.

The Beeching proposals were rushed into effect, and on Saturday, 4th April, 1964, the threatened Melton to Sheringham line was closed. A few months prior to this, in April 1963, the western arm of the triangle between Newstead Lane Junction and Runton West Junction had been axed, and this meant that all trains between Norwich and Sheringham had to run in and out of Cromer, with a reversal at Cromer Beach.

The closures of 1963–64 left the Sheringham to Cromer Beach line in splendid isolation as the north-western extremity of a long branch line from Norwich Thorpe. This was not, however, the end of the rationalisation process, for the lavish facilities at Cromer and Sheringham were still considered to be over-elaborate in relation to modern (i.e. much reduced) traffic needs. In January 1967 the Norwich to Sheringham line was reduced to conductor-guard operation, with a dmu-worked service calling at unstaffed halts; all tickets were issued on the trains, and most cheap tickets and through booking facilities were withdrawn. At Sheringham, the former M& GN station was closed altogether, and in its place BR erected a simple halt on the eastern side of Station Road. This new facility was opened to the public on 2nd January, 1967, on which date the old station was taken out of use.

The Post-Beeching Years

In October 1964 the Conservative Government had been replaced by a Labour administration, and this change of government led to a changed attitude towards mass railway closures. The Beeching programme was brought to an end, and many commentators predicted that no Labour government would ever implement the kind of large-scale closure plan implicit in the Beeching proposals. Unfortunately, the new government's transport policy was not as sympathetic towards railways as it appeared, and although Transport Minister Barbara Castle's policies enabled 'socially-necessary' routes to be subsidised by local or national government, the majority of these favoured lines were (perhaps by chance) in Labour areas. Conversely, the Labour proposals envisaged that many lines in rural, predominately Tory areas, would be excluded from the 'basic network', and this resulted in a curious situation whereby many branch lines that had escaped the initial axe were earmarked for closure; plans published in 1967 purported to show a basic system of around 11,000 route miles – but closer examination revealed that the Norwich–Cromer–Sheringham line would probably not be included in the nationalised system.

At the beginning of 1968 BR posted closure notices for several East Anglian branch lines – among them the Cromer and Sheringham route. Happily, Norwich to Sheringham services were eventually reprieved, and having narrowly escaped closure in 1968–69, this surviving section of the once-extensive M&GN–GER lines in north Norfolk was awarded a 3-year grant of £133,000 under Section 39 of the 1968 Transport Act.

The Sheringham to Cromer Beach branch therefore remained in being as part of a 30½ mile local route from Norwich and, as a recipient of grant aid, the line still supported a relatively frequent train service of around 12/13 trains each way. In May 1972, for instance, there were nine trains each way between Sheringham and Norwich, together with three up and three down workings between Norwich and Cromer. One summer Saturday through service remained, and this solitary working departed from Liverpool Street at 10.04 am and reached Sheringham by 2.07 pm. In the reverse direction, the corresponding up service left Sheringham at 2.42 pm and, having called at Cromer, the train – usually a six car class '101' dmu formation – arrived back in London by 6.22 pm.

Freight traffic was handled at Cromer Beach until the early 1970s, but by 1980 the freight service from Norwich had been cut back to North Walsham (where an oil depot and other industries ensured a supply of bulk traffic for the line).

The cessation of goods traffic and the withdrawal of all locomotive-hauled trains allowed the 3¾ miles of line between Cromer Beach and Sheringham to be worked on the 'basic railway' principle with no loops, sidings or other connections on the single line. The stations at West Runton and Sheringham (BR) were merely halts, but Cromer managed to retain at least some of its Victorian infrastructure. The large station buildings remained intact – albeit not in railway use – while two platforms and two terminal roads were available for use when up and down multiple unit trains were required to pass each other. The Norwich and Sheringham lines were worked as two parallel single lines although, to the casual observer, there still appeared to be a double track exit from the station.

Although the 3¾ miles of former M&GN line between Cromer Beach and Sheringham had been retained as part of the modern BR system the route had, to some extent, lost much of its Midland & Great Northern atmosphere – the branch was after all now a part of the rival GER network! On the other hand, the line had at least remained in being, and it thus fared much better than the M&GN main line from Great Yarmouth to the Midlands. Happily, local enthusiasts felt that the M&GN system warranted some form of pre-servation, and, as far back as May 1959, advertisements were placed in the *Railway Magazine* to see what support might be available for such a project.

Table 51 — MELTON CONSTABLE, SHERINGHAM and CROMER

Week Days

Miles		am H W	am	am 5 Y	am	am F	am	am S E	am	am	am	am B Y A	noon H S	pm	pm C	pm	pm	pm	pm T P	pm	pm Y	pm T S E	pm	pm R S	Sundays pm Y X U	pm Y	pm Y
—	Melton Constable.. dep	5 45	6 50	7 28			9 35	9 39	10 2	10 33	11 21	11 38	12 17	1 35	3 52		4 54	6 0		8 10	9 3	10 34	11 36	258 0		4 43
5	Holt	6	57				9 53	10 42	10			11 48	12 23		4 0		4 1	6 10		8 20	9 9	10 40	11 46	258 8		4 51
8¼	Weybourne			7 30			10 2	10 54	10			11 56	12 10		4 8		4 1	6 18		8 28	9 13	10 44	11 53	41 14		4 57
11¼	Sheringham.. {arr	6 7	7 36				9 23	10 8	11			12 5	12 26		4 24			6 24		8 34	9 15	10 51		61 16		5 4
	{dep	6	7 40				9 27	10 13				12 12	12 30		4 30			6 30		8 47	9 22	10 58		101 20		5 4
13	West Runton	7	44				10 18					12 14	12		4 35			6 36		8 52	9 30	11 2 6		151 25		5 9
15	Cromer (Beach) arr	6 15	7 49				9 32	10 18	11			12 21	1 02		4 12			6 47			9 39	11 21 5				

Week Days (return)

Miles		am R	am J	am	am T L G	am	am	am	am	noon H S D	pm M	pm S E	pm K P	pm S E	pm	pm	pm Y	pm	pm Y	pm T T S E	pm	Sundays pm Y	pm Y
—	Cromer (Beach) .... dep		7 50	8 40	9 29		10 1	1034		12 17	1 35	2 29	3 50	4 1	4 54			6 39		7 20	9 3		2 24	
2	West Runton		7 56	8 46	9 49		10	1040		1223	1 41	3 36	3 56		4 4			6 46		7 26	9 9		2 30	
3¾	Sheringham.. {arr		7 59	8 49	9 53			1046		1226	1 47	3 8 14	4 1		4 14			6 57		7 29	9 13		2 34	
	{dep		8 2	8 57			10	1053		1228		2 40 16			4					7 30	9 15		2 36	
6¾	Weybourne		8 7	9 1			10	1058			12 0	2 50 31	4 85		4 6			6 49		7 37	9 22		2 43	
10	Holt	7	8 12	9 9			10 3	11 2 6		12 0	1246	2 58	4 16		4			6 57		7 45	9 30		2 50	
15	Melton Constable.. arr	7 448	8 26	9 16			10 3018	11 21 55		1217	1255	7¾ 40	4 25		4			7 6		7 54	9 39			

A Saturdays only and not after 1st September
B Through Carriages from Leicester (London Road) (Table 50)
C On Saturdays until 8th September. On Sats. from Derby (Mid.) (Table 50) Sats. only. Runs 30th June to 25th Aug incl.
D Except Saturdays
E On Saturdays Through Train to Liverpool Street
F
G On Mondays to Fridays; also Saturdays 16th, and 23rd June. Through Carriages to Birmingham (New Street) (Table 50)
H Through Carriages from or to Shirebrook W.
J On Sats. until 8th Sept. incl. Thro' Carriages from or to Birmingham (New St.) (Table 50)
K Through Carriages to Leicester (London Road) (Table 50)
L Saturdays only. Commences 30th June

M On Saturdays 30th June to 8th September inclusive. Through Carriages to Peterborough (North)
P Saturdays only and not after 8th Sept
R From or to Norwich (City) (Table 46)
S Saturdays only
T Through Carriages to or from Birmingham (New Street) (Table 50)
U Runs 1st July to 9th September inclusive
V Runs 24th June to 9th September inclusive
W Saturdays only. Runs 30th June to 25th June to 25th August inclusive
X Runs 17th, 24th June & 16th Sept. only
Y Through Carriages to or from London (Liverpool Street) (Table 46)
Z Mondays, Fridays, and Saturdays
For **OTHER TRAINS** between Sheringham and Cromer, see **Table 46**

A British Railways timetable for 11th June, 1956 until 16th September, 1956.

A British Railways timetable for 1st May, 1972 to 6th May, 1973, including the line to Sheringham.

Second class only

4 LONDON LIVERPOOL ST. / IPSWICH — NORWICH — CROMER — SHERINGHAM

Miles												
—	4 LONDON LIVERPOOL ST.	d										
—	4 IPSWICH	d										
—	NORWICH	d										
6	SALHOUSE	d										
8½	WROXHAM	d										
13	WORSTEAD	d										
16	NORTH WALSHAM	d										
19	GUNTON	d										
24	CROMER	a										
28	WEST RUNTON											
30½	SHERINGHAM	a										

SHERINGHAM — CROMER — NORWICH — IPSWICH — LONDON LIVERPOOL ST. (Sundays)

Miles												
—	SHERINGHAM	d										
—	WEST RUNTON	d										
—	CROMER	d										
10½	GUNTON	d										
14½	NORTH WALSHAM	d										
17½	WORSTEAD	d										
21½	WROXHAM	d										
24	SALHOUSE	d										
30½	NORWICH	a										
7¾	4 IPSWICH	a										
145	4 LONDON LIVERPOOL ST.	a										

Holt Level Crossing and Signal Box (now at Weybourne on NNR) just one week prior to closure. *Tom Carr*

Holt Station looking East just one week prior to closure in 1964. *Tom Carr*

The initial scheme evoked an encouraging response, and in October 1959, the Midland & Great Northern Society was formed at a meeting held in Great Yarmouth.

The North Norfolk Railway

The M & GN Society hoped, at first, to be able to revive the Yarmouth to North Walsham line, but this project was abandoned when the County Council announced that the trackbed would be needed for a new road. Attention then switched to the Norwich City branch, but there were, in this case, insurmountable problems insofar as BR needed the line for freight traffic. Finally, in 1965, a company known as Central Norfolk Enterprises was formed with the aim of re-opening the Melton Constable to Sheringham line. Regrettably, new road schemes prevented the company from proceeding with its original plans for a line to Melton, but it was later possible for the preservationists to purchase a section of line between Golf Links Crossing (near Sheringham) and Weybourne station.

The closure of Sheringham BR station in January 1967 enabled the company to establish its headquarters in the former M & GN station, and in the next few months the near-derelict offices and waiting rooms were adapted for use as a transport museum. There was still much to do before the line could be re-opened, but in the interim a variety of preserved locomotives and rolling stock were placed on public display. The most impressive exhibits, at this formative stage, were 'B12' 4–6–0 No. 61572 and 'J15' 0–6–0 No. 65462; a four-coach Gresley 'Quad-art' articulated set was available for use on the line, while, in the hope that an all-year-round train service could one day be provided, there were also two ex-BR four-wheel railbuses. These interesting vehicles had been built by the German firm of Waggon und Maschinenbau, and their BR numbers were E79960 and E79963; both units were soon put to work as lightweight locomotives during weekend restoration work.

There was much work ahead before the line could be opened for the carriage of passenger traffic, and in the ensuing years there were several organisational changes at Sheringham. In February 1971, Central Norfolk Enterprises was reborn as the aptly-named 'North Norfolk Railway' and, following the lead taken by other preservation groups, the supporters of the scheme organised themselves into two mutually-supporting bodies; the stations, trackwork and other essential infrastructure were owned by the North Norfolk Railway, and this public limited company was supported by the Midland & Great Northern Joint Railway Society, which assisted the owning company in a variety of ways.

The 2¾ mile line between Sheringham and Weybourne was worked on a 'members only' basis until May 1976, but thereafter the railway was worked under a Light Railway Order. In the meantime, additional rolling stock continued to arrive at Sheringham station and, despite the tarring-over of the level crossing between the BR and North Norfolk stations, some at least of these extra vehicles were delivered by rail. On 16th March, 1975 the last such delivery was made, when five passenger vehicles and a van were propelled to Sheringham by a BR class '31' A1A-A1A locomotive; at Sheringham, the stock was shunted delicately over a temporary connection that had been installed by volunteer labour. In this way, the North Norfolk line gained several useful coaches – including two former 'Brighton Belle' Pullman cars (the other three passenger vehicles were Eastern Region suburban stock).

In 1986, the North Norfolk line carried 122,343 passengers, while further income accrued from the sale of books, souvenirs and other items. Like other preserved lines, the NNR has featured in several period film and television programmes, notably the 1940's *Dad's Army*, the 1950's holiday camp comedy series *Hi De Hi!*, and, more recently portraying the 1970's in a Ruth Rendell mystery.

As a tourist attraction, the North Norfolk line undoubtedly benefited from its location in the popular north Norfolk coastal area, but the original 2 mile 55 chain section between Sheringham and Weybourne was somewhat short in relation to other preserved railways. Road construction in the Holt area prevented an extension of the NNR into Holt itself, but it was possible for the route to be prolonged for a little over 3 miles to a new station on the edge of Holt. The necessary Light Railway Order was obtained in 1987; the line had already been extended beyond Weybourne station to a halt at Kelling Heath (3 miles from Sheringham), and the LRO permitted an extension beyond this point to the projected terminus at Holt, at the point where the junction for the proposed branch to Blakeney would have been – a total distance of 5 miles. The track on this section was relayed between 1981 and 1987.

The Holt extension was obviously an important objective for the North Norfolk Railway, but much important work had also been carried out on the original 2¾ mile section from Sheringham to Weybourne. The two stations were thoroughly renovated, the transformation at Weybourne being particularly noticeable because this once-remote place was chosen as the site of the NNR's fully-equipped sheds and workshops. The works was opened in 1980, and this new facility was soon carrying out major rebuilding and renovation projects; in 1982, for instance, the works turned out its first vehicle in the form of a former LNER varnished teak Gresley buffet car 51769.

The locomotive and rolling stock fleet on the North Norfolk line now includes a variety of engines, carriages and wagons from the LNER/Eastern Region and other sources. The original 'B12' and 'J15' locomotives provide a nucleus of suitable ex-British Rail types, while the articulated 'Quad-art' set, the Eastern Region suburban coaches and the Gresley buffet car contribute further 'local' flavour. Whilst unfortunately the preservation movement came too late to save any authentic M&GN locomotives, the body of M&GN (ex-GN third) No. 129 a 6 wheeled wooden bodied coach was recently discovered and removed to Sheringham for restoration.

The two 'Brighton Belle' Pullman cars are, in a sense, less suitable for use on the North Norfolk line, but they are, nonetheless, popular attractions that add an element of romance to the NNR line. The two German-built railbuses operate on lightly-used services – one of their regular duties, around 1987,

GER class Y14 No. 564 brings the first public steam hauled passenger train to a stand at the new Holt station on 19th March, 1989.

Steve Allen

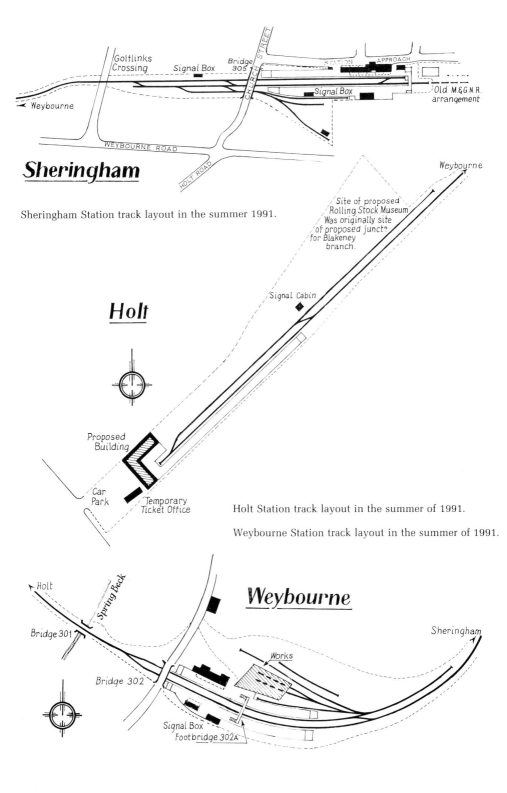

Sheringham

Golflinks Crossing
Signal Box
Bridge 305
CHURCH STREET
STATION APPROACH
Old M.&G.N.R. arrangement
Signal Box
Weybourne
WEYBOURNE ROAD
HOLT ROAD

Sheringham Station track layout in the summer 1991.

Weybourne

Site of proposed Rolling Stock Museum. Was originally site of proposed junctⁿ for Blakeney branch.

Holt

Signal Cabin

Proposed Building

Car Park
Temporary Ticket Office

Holt Station track layout in the summer of 1991.

Weybourne Station track layout in the summer of 1991.

Holt
Spring Beck
Weybourne
Sheringham
Bridge 301
Works
Bridge 302
Signal Box
Footbridge 302ᴬ

being a short-distance shuttle working between Weybourne station and the then western terminus at Kelling Camp Halt.

Like other preserved lines the North Norfolk Railway has realised the value of former industrial locomotives, which use less fuel than their main line counterparts and (when fitted with vacuum brakes) are ideally-suited for everyday usage on a light railway. The NNR's industrial locos include Hunslet 0-6-0STs No. 1982 'Ring Haw', Austerity No. 3809 and Andrew Barclay 0-6-0T 'Harlaxton'.

Table 6

NORTH NORFOLK RAILWAY MOTIVE POWER 1991

Type	Wheelbase	Notes
Holden 'B12' class	4-6-0	No. 61572 – in Holland for restoration
Worsdell 'J15' class	0-6-0	No. 65462 – awaiting restoration
LMS 3F	0-6-0T	No. 47383 – on loan from Severn Valley Railway
Hunslet	0-6-0ST	No. 1982 – *Ring Haw*
Hunslet Austerity	0-6-0ST	No. 3809
Peckett	0-6-0ST	No. 1970 – *John D. Hammer* sold Sept 91
Barclay	0-6-0T	No. 2107 – *Harlaxton* rest completed 91
Bagnall	0-6-0	No. 2370 – (fireless) on display
Bagnall	0-6-0ST	*Birchenwood* – awaiting restoration
Robert Stephenson	0-6-0T	No. 12 – on display
Hudswell, Clarke	0-6-0ST	No. 1700 – *Wissington* on display
Hawthorn, Leslie	0-4-0ST	No. 2918 – *Pony* awaiting restoration
Barclay	0-4-0ST	Edmondsons – out of use
BR Darlington	0-6-0	No. 12131 – Class 11
BRCW	Bo-Bo	No. D5386 – Class 27 (ex No. 27066)
BR Derby	Bo-Bo	No. 25027 – Class 25 (ex No. D5207)
English Electric	0-4-0	No. 10
Ruston Hornsby	0-4-0DM	Nicknamed *Tipockety*
Waggon-Maschinenbau	DRB 4W	E79960 – under restoration
Waggon-Maschinenbau	DRB 4W	E79963

Table 7

NORTH NORFOLK RAILWAY COACHING STOCK c.1991

No.	Rly	Type	Date	Builder	Owner
295	GER	Corridor Brake Third (LNER/BR 62377 dept. DE320325)	1907	GER Stratford	M&GNJRS
1	L&YR	Directors Saloon (LMS 10701, 45037 BR M45037M)	1908	L&YR Newton Heath	M&GNJRS
5318	LNWR	Directors Saloon (LMS 10500, 45002 BR M45002M)	1913	LNWR Wolverton	M&GNJRS

No.	Rly	Type	Date	Builder	Owner
Set 74	LNER	Quad Art Set (LNER Nos. 48941/2/3/4 BR Nos. E86762/3/4/5E)	1924	LNER Doncaster	Carriage & Wagon Trust
771	LNER	BY (4 wheel Pigeon Van) (BR dept E040923E)	1929	LNER York	Private P. McOwan
s 3395	LNER	Corridor Third (TK)	1931	Metro-Cammel Wednesbury	M&GNJRS
s 87	Pullman Car Co.	Brighton Belle Parlour Car	1931	Metro-Cammel Saltley	Private & NNR
s 91	Pullman Car Co	Brighton Belle Driving Parlour Car	1931	Metro-Cammel Saltley	Private & NNR
s 51769	LNER	Buffet Restaurant Car (RB) (BR E9128E)	1937	LNER York	M&GNJRS
70621	LNER	(Thompson) Bogie Brake (BG) 'Austerity' design wooden planked not teak panels	1945	LNER York	M&GNJRS
624	LMS	Third class sleeper (SLSTP) BR W624M	1951	BR Derby	NNR
s E3868	BR	Tourist Second Open (TSO)	1951	BR York	NNR
s E4521	BR	" "	1956	BR York	NNR
s E4651	BR	" "	1957	BR York	NNR
s E4355	BR	" "	1956	BRCW (Avon Valley Railway on leave to NNR)	
M4843	BR	" "	1959	BR Wolverton	NNR
s E21103	BR	Brake Corridor Composite (BCK)	1956	Metro-Cammel Saltley	NNR
s M81033	BR	Gangwayed Brake (converted to Kitchen Car) (BG)	1961	BR	NNR
s 581269	BR	Gangwayed Brake (BG)	1957	Pressed Steel	Private
s E43034	BR	Suburban Composite Lavatory (CL)	1954	BR Doncaster	NNR
s E43041	BR	" "	1954	BR Doncaster	NNR
E43357	BR	Suburban Brake Second (BS) (Brake being converted to generator car 1991)	1954	BR York	NNR
s E43359	BR	" "	1955	BR York	NNR
E46147	BR	Suburban Second (S)	1954	BR Wolverton	NNR
E48026	BR	Suburban Second Lavatory Open (SLO) (converted to flat wagon 1988)	1955	BR Doncaster	NNR

Freight stock is of a typically varied nature, with a representative selection of open wagons, ventilated vans, oil tank wagons and a former Southern Railway brake van. Quite apart from their intrinsic interest as historic rolling stock, these freight vehicles are sometimes used during ballasting or other engineering work – for which purpose the NNR use diesel shunter Class 11. The NNR also own two diminutive diesel locos which are used for pilot duties and some winter works trains.

Future plans for the NNR are to build a replica M&GN station at Holt, incorporating all the necessary visitor amenities, and a carriage restoration workshop at Weybourne, they are also intending to restore the J15 locomotive as soon as funds allow. The M&GNJRS intention, following restoration of the B12 locomotive in Holland, is to build a rolling stock museum on site

LMS 3F, No. 47383 (on loan from Severn Valley Railway for 1991 season) pulls out of Sheringham station past Sheringham West signal box (ex-Wensum Junction Norwich) on 20th July, 1991. *Steve Allen*

Diesel Railbus No. E79963 pauses at Kelling Heath Park Halt in May 1989. *Steve Allen*

Peckett 0–6–0ST No. 1970 *John D. Hammer* storms out of Weybourne up Kelling Bank on 3rd February, 1991 with a Pullman Luncheon special. *Steve Allen*

LMS 3F No. 47383 storms the 1-80 gradient of Kelling Bank with a train for Holt on 20th July, 1991. This piece of line is considered by many to be the most scenic in East Anglia. *Steve Allen*

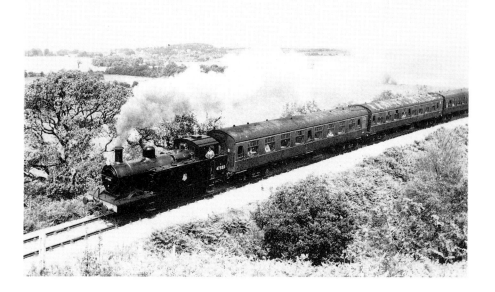

Hunslet 'Austerity' No. 3809 coasts into Weybourne station with a Pullman Sunday Lunch special on 9th September, 1990   *Steve Allen*

LNER J72 No. 69023 runs around its train at Sheringham on 14th August, 1989.
Steve Allen

at Holt. The Midland and Great Northern Joint Railway Society is the supporting society for the North Norfolk Railway, if you are interested in becoming a member please write to: The Membership Secretary, M&GNJRS c/o Sheringham Station, Sheringham, Norfolk. If you are interested in becoming a shareholder in the NNR, please write to the same address, addressing your letter to North Norfolk Railway plc.

Postscript: The Melton to Cromer Line Today

In its heyday the Midland & Great Northern branch from Melton Constable to Cromer Beach encompassed 15¼ miles of line. Today, no less than 9 miles remain in use, the 3¾ mile section between Cromer and Sheringham (BR) being part of the national railway system, while a further 5 miles between Sheringham and Holt are operated by the North Norfolk Railway between March and November. The extant parts of the Melton to Cromer line are remarkably intact, with three relatively large stations at Cromer Beach, Sheringham and Weybourne which remain as visible reminders of the former M&GN system.

It is, of course, important to remember that the North Norfolk Railway and the surviving BR line between Cromer and Sheringham are very different undertakings. The NNR only runs during the summer, and its infrastructure is geared to the needs of holidaymakers rather than everyday travellers, although it provides a service for some local people who use it to avoid congestion in Sheringham on market days. The BR line, in contrast, has been pared to the bone – yet this severely-rationalised route sustains an all-year-round service comparable, in terms of frequency, to that provided in M&GN days!

The May 1989 timetable consisted of 13 up and 13 down workings between Sheringham and Norwich, one morning train – the 6.25 am ex-Sheringham – being a through service to Birmingham New Street; the latter working ran via Peterborough and Leicester, and can be seen as a successor to the famous M&GN 'Leicesters' of years gone by. Cromer Beach had, by 1989, declined in importance as an intermediate passing place on the Norwich to Sheringham route, although some morning and evening services still passed there (other workings crossed at North Walsham, on the former GER Cromer–Norwich line). The Sunday service provided five up and five down trains each way between Norwich and Sheringham, journey times, on both weekdays and Sundays, being just over one hour for the 30¼ mile, stopping train journey through rural Norfolk. In 1991 Cromer Beach station yard was being redeveloped as housing and shops. The platforms have been severed between the bay platforms and the buildings to allow an access road to the new development.

An innovation, in recent years, has been the availability of through booking facilities between the BR and North Norfolk lines. It is also encouraging to note that North Norfolk timetables are now printed in BR timetables, and this will, perhaps, enable the NNR to portray itself as a provider of public transport facilities – as well as a highly-successful working museum railway.

Notes

1. William Marriott, *Forty Years of a Norfolk Railway* (1974).
2. *op. cit.*
3. PRO MT6 files.
4. PRO MT6 files.
5. Marriott, *op. cit.*
6. The air defence of Great Britain during World War I was entrusted to the Royal Naval Air Service, and much useful data relating to that period can be found in the extensive archives now held at the Fleet Air Arm Museum, RNAS Yeovilton.
7. R.S. McNaught, Lost Railway: Memories of the M & GN, *Meccano Magazine*, Vol 44, September 1959, pp. 392–94, 420.
8. See letter in the November 1966 *Railway World*, p. 486.
9. *The Railway Magazine*, July 1930.
10. *The Railway Magazine*, February 1933.
11. See *The Fairford Branch* (1985) by S.C. Jenkins.
12. Edgar J. March, *Inshore Craft of Great Britain*, Vol 1 (1970).
13. PRO MT6 files.
14. PRO MT6 files.

Other sources are, in general, mentioned in the text; these include Acts, official documents, E & MR Directors' reports, and contemporary journals such as *The Railway Times*, *The Locomotive Magazine*, *The Engineer*, *The Railway Magazine* and *The Railway Engineer*.

Hunslet 0–6–0ST No. 1980 *Ring Haw* runs into Weybourne station under the newly erected (ex-Stowmarket) footbridge in May 1990.   *Steve Allen*

Appendix One
Chronological List of Important Dates

1845	Projected North of Norfolk Railway (Norwich to Holt).
1846	Proposed Norfolk Railway extension to Blakeney.
1862	Creation of Great Eastern Railway.
1876	Incorporation of Lynn & Fakenham Railway in opposition to GER (13th July).
1877	East Norfolk Railway reaches Cromer (26th March).
1880	Lynn & Fakenham empowered to build lines to Norwich & Blakeney (12th August).
1881	Lynn & Fakenham obtains Powers to build line to Cromer (11th August).
1882	Lynn & Fakenham line opened to Melton and Guestwick (19th January).
	Lynn & Fakenham obtains Powers to deviate Blakeney line (11th August).
	Formation of Eastern & Midlands Railway (18th August).
1883	Lynn & Fakenham amalgamated with Eastern & Midlands Railway (1st January).
	Work on Cromer line temporarily abandoned.
1884	Line opened from Melton Constable to Holt (1st October).
1885	Works on Holt to Cromer line in abeyance.
1886	Construction resumes.
1887	Completion of line from Holt to Cromer Beach (16th June).
1888	Eastern & Midlands obtains Powers to abandon Blakeney line (28th June).
1893	The Great Northern introduces its 'Cromer Express' in opposition to GER.
1894	Formation of Midland & Great Northern Railways Joint Committee (9th June).
1897	Changes at Sheringham station.
1898	Formation of Norfolk & Suffolk Joint Committee (M&GN & GER).
1901	New station opened at Weybourne (1st July).
	Proposed light railway from Sheringham to Blakeney.
1902	Through Cromer to Leicester trains become all-year-round service.
1906	Opening of Cromer to Mundesley line (GER 23rd July: M&GN 3rd August).
	Opening of new facilities at Sheringham (in connection with above).
	The Norfolk Coast Express starts running to Sheringham.
1923	Grouping of main line railways; M&GN owned by LMS and LNER companies.
1936	M&GN passes into LNER control; Melton works closed as major repair centre.
1939	Train services curtailed on outbreak of World War II.
1943	Through train to Liverpool Street restored.
1948	Nationalisation of Railway system (1st January).
1953	Cromer to Mundesley branch closed (6th April).
1954	Great Eastern line trains diverted to Cromer Beach (19th September).
1958	Most of M&GN system closed (28th February).
1959	Reduction of through working onto Cromer/Sheringham line.
1963	Newstead Lane–Runton West spur closed (April).
1964	Melton–Sheringham line closed to all traffic (4th April).
1967	Norwich–Sheringham route reduced to conductor-guard operation (January).
	Sheringham station replaced by simple halt (2nd January).
1968	Closure proposals for Norwich–Cromer–Sheringham line.
1976	North Norfolk Railway obtains Light Railway Order.
1981	North Norfolk Railway opens works at Weybourne.
1985	First 'Pacer' unit reaches Cromer and Sheringham (November).
1987	North Norfolk Railway obtains Light Railway Order for Holt extension.

Appendix Two
Facilities at Cromer Beach and Intermediate Stations

Melton Constable
Island platform (800 ft)
Booking office/waiting rooms/refreshment room
Private waiting room for Lord Hastings
Extensive goods yard
Coal, watering and locomotive facilities (including 3-road shed)
Locomotive, carriage & wagon works
Locomotive turntable
Cattle dock
1 ton fixed hand crane
Gas works (railway-owned)
2 signal cabins
Permanent way huts & stores, etc.
Railway staff housing, school, etc.

Holt
Up and down passenger platforms
Passing loop
Booking office/waiting rooms
Subsidiary accommodation on up platform
Signal cabin
Level crossing
Goods yard
Huts, permanent way sheds, goods lock-up, etc.
Cattle pens and loading docks

Weybourne
Up and down platforms (each 350 ft long)
Passing loop (400 yds)
Booking office/waiting room
Waiting shelter on up platform
Signal cabin (20 levers)
2 goods sidings
Loading docks and cattle pens

Sheringham
Up and down platforms
Bay platform
Passing loop
Booking office/waiting rooms/toilets etc.
Subsidiary accommodation on up platform
2 signal cabins

Lattice girder footbridge
Level crossing
Goods loop and headshunt
5 goods sidings
Limited locomotive facilities for visiting GER locomotives
Mess room and office for Great Eastern staff
Cattle dock
Loading dock
Permanent way huts, sheds, etc.

Cromer Beach
Main terminal platform (extended to over 800 ft in BR period)
Branch bay platform (340 ft)
Booking office/waiting rooms/toilets etc.
Refreshment rooms
Overall roof (176 25 ft)
Run-round facilities
Carriage and marshalling sidings (4) plus short spur behind signal cabin)
Goods sidings (4)
Single road locomotive shed
65 ft diameter locomotive turntable
Ashpit and coaling stage
Office, mess room, etc. for locomotive crews
Goods shed
Weigh-house
Stables for shunting and dray horses
Private siding to Cromer Electricity Works
Private siding to Cromer Gas Works (between Cromer and West Runton)
Coal wharves, storage sheds, etc. for local coal merchants
Grain stores (in goods yard beside goods shed)
Fish store (small shed on passenger platform)
Goods offices
Signal cabin (ultimately 35 levers)
Lamp room, cycle sheds, etc.
Permanent way hut
Cattle pens
1 ton fixed hand crane

Bibliography

The literature of the M&GN is quite extensive, but books or articles relating to the Cromer branch (or other specific parts of the system) are comparatively rare. It follows that many of the works listed below are of a peripheral nature, but they may, nevertheless, be of interest to those seeking further information on locomotives or other aspects of the Midland & Great Northern Railway.

A.J. Wrottesley, The Midland & Great Northern Joint Railway (1970).

H.C. Casserley, Britain's Joint Lines (1968).

William Marriott, Forty Years of a Norfolk Railway (1974).

G.A. Sekon, Railways in Poppyland, Railway Magazine, June 1898.

V.R. Webster, Train Working at Cromer, Railway Magazine, September 1954.

M.J. Clark, The Norfolk & Suffolk Joint Railway, GERS Journal, June 1980.

V.L. Whitechurch, Cromer, Railway Magazine, June 1898.

E. Tuddenham, The M&GN Route to Cromer, Railway World, June 1964.

—— The Norfolk & Suffolk Joint, Railway World, July 1966.

Ronald H. Clark, A Short History of the Midland & Great Northern Jt. Railway (1967).

Stanley C. Jenkins, The Lynn & Hunstanton Railway (1987).

—— The Cromer Branch (1989).

*J.H. Farrington, Melton Constable, Railway Modeller, November 1980.

R.S. McNaught, Lost Railway: Memories of the M&GNJ, Meccano Magazine, September 1959.

*D.R. Featherstone, M&GNR 0–6–0T (LNER class J93) Model Railway Constructor, April 1971.

*Ken Werrett, Midland & Great Northern 8-ton Low Sided Wagon, Railway Modeller, December 1974.

Ronald H. Clarke, Scenes from the Midland & Great Northern Joint Railway (1978).

*T.A. Lindsay, Johnson's Standard 0–4–4 Tank, Model Railway News, December 1962.

*T.A. Lindsay, Midland Railway 0–6–0 Class M, Model Railway News, March 1961.

*†Bill Ibbott, SDJR 4–4–0s, Railway Modeller, June 1968 (cf. M&GN 4–4–0s).

*†Bill Ibbott & D. Jenkinson, Beautiful Beatrice, Railway Modeller, April 1965.

Articles marked * contain scale plans of interest to modellers of the M&GN Cromer branch. The two articles marked † deal with Johnson standard 4–4–0s, the S&DJR version being a small-wheeled version while the 'Beatrice' type had 7 ft coupled wheels; the M&GN class 'C' engines had 6 ft 6 in. wheels, but they were otherwise similar to the S&DJR/Midland version, and the two articles listed should thus be of help to potential model-makers.

Index